ANTIWORLDS

Translated by

W. H. AUDEN

JEAN GARRIGUE

MAX HAYWARD

STANLEY KUNITZ

STANLEY MOSS

WILLIAM JAY SMITH

RICHARD WILBUR

Poetry by

ANTIWORLDS

ANDREI VOZNESENSKY

Edited by PATRICIA BLAKE and MAX HAYWARD

With a Foreword by W. H. AUDEN

BASIC BOOKS, INC., Publishers   New York

FOREWORD

It is, of course, sheer folly to imagine that one can pass judgments which are either accurate or just upon poems written in a language which one does not know.

Irrespective of their relative merits, some poets lose less in translation than others. Even in the crudest prose translation a non-Italian reader can immediately recognize that Dante is a great poet, because much of the impact of his poetry depends upon his use of similes and metaphors drawn from sensory experiences which are not confined to Italians but common to all peoples, and upon his gift for aphoristic statements expressed in the simplest everyday words for which every language has a more or less exact equivalent: e.g., "That day we read in it no further."

Translation also favors poets like Hölderlin and Smart, who were dotty, for their dislocation of normal processes of thinking are the result of their dottiness not their language, and sound equally surprising in any: e.g., ". . . now the heroes are dead, the islands of Love are almost disfigured. Thus everywhere must Love be tricked and exploited, silly."

A poet like Campion, on the other hand, whose principal concern is with the sound of words and their metrical and rhythmical relations, cannot be translated at all. Take away the English language in which his songs were written, and all that remains are a few banal sentiments.

The most notorious case of an untranslatable poet is Pushkin. Russians are unanimous in regarding him as their greatest poet, but I have yet to read a translation which, if I did not know this, would lead me to suppose that his poems had any merit whatsoever.

Complete ignorance, however, is perhaps less likely to lead one's critical judgment astray than a smattering of a language. Ignorance at least knows it does not know. When one recalls the fantastic overestimation of Ossian by the German Romantics or of Poe by Baudelaire and Mallarmé, one thinks twice before expressing enthusiasm for a foreign poet.

In the case of Mr. Voznesensky, at least I know that he is greatly admired by many of his fellow countrymen, and, after reading literal prose translations of his poems, studying metrical models, and listening to tape recordings of him reading his own work, I am convinced that his admirers are right.

As a fellow maker, I am struck first and foremost by his craftsmanship. Here, at least, is a poet who knows that, whatever else it may be, a poem is a verbal artifact which must be as skillfully and solidly constructed as a table or a motorcycle. Whatever effects can be secured in Russian by rhythm, rhyme, assonance, and contrasts of diction, he clearly knows all about. For example:

v

Vcherá moi dóktor proiznyós:	(a)
"Talánt v vas, mózhet, i vozmózhen,	(b)
no vásh payál'nik obmorózhen,	(b)
ne súites' íz-domu v moróz."	(a)
O nós . . .	(a)

(Yesterday my doctor declared:
"Talent in you, perhaps there may be
but your blow torch is frozen,
don't go out of the house in the cold."
Oh nose . . .)

Toi priróde, molchál'no-chúdnoi,	(assonance)
róshcha, ózero li, brevnó—	(b)
im pozvóleno slúshat', chúvstvovat',	(assonance)
tól'ko gólosa im ne danó.	(b)

(Nature, silent and wonderful
forest, lake, or log—
is only permitted to listen and feel.
It has not been granted a voice.)

Effects like the introduction of a slang word for nose in the middle of more conventional diction can be reproduced more or less in another language, but Mr. Voznesensky's metrical effects must make any translator despair. Russian verse seems to be predominantly trochaic or dactylic, whereas English falls naturally into iambic or anapaestic patterns.

Obvious, too, at a glance is the wide range of subject matter by which Mr. Voznesensky is imaginatively excited—he is equally interested in animals and airports, native and alien landscapes—and the variety of tones, elegiac, comic, grotesque, quiet, rebellious, which he can command.

Lastly, every word he writes, even when he is criticizing, reveals a profound love for his native land and its traditions. I wish to stress this strongly because, given the existing political climate, there is a danger that we shall misunderstand him by looking for ideological clues instead of reading his poems as one would read any poet who is a fellow countryman.

The meaning of any poem is the result of a dialogue between the words on the page and the particular person who happens to be reading it—that is to say, to no two readers is its meaning identical. Our social and historical memories as Americans or Englishmen are quite different from those of a Russian. To mention only one difference, poets in our countries have never been considered socially important enough for the state to take any notice of them, to encourage or discourage, finance or censor, whereas in Russia, whatever the regime, they have been taken seriously. But it is only in terms of our own experience that we can profitably read Mr. Voznesensky. If we should attempt to read him as if we were members of his Russian audience, our interpretations will almost certainly be wide of the mark. Besides being foolish, such an attempt is quite unnecessary. One of the primary proofs that a poem, or any work of art, has value is that, wherever, whenever, and by whomever it was made, we find it relevant to ourselves, our time, and our place. I am certain that Mr. Voznesensky is a good poet because, though I know no Russian and have never been to Russia, his poems, even in English translation, have much to say to me.

W. H. Auden

INTRODUCTION

Andrei Voznesensky, Russia's foremost modern poet, was born in Moscow on May 12, 1933. Part of his early childhood was spent in the ancient Russian city of Vladimir. During the war, from 1941 to 1944, he lived with his mother in Kurgan, in the Urals, while his father, a professor of engineering in peacetime, was in Leningrad, engaged in evacuating factories during the blockade.

Both Voznesensky's parents have literary and artistic interests. His mother read poetry to him from his earliest childhood—Severyanin and Pasternak, he remembers in particular. Voznesensky recalls seeing his father once during the war when he flew to Kurgan on leave from the front. He carried nothing with him but a small rucksack containing some food and a little book of reproductions of etchings by Goya which powerfully affected his small son. Voznesensky's childhood apprehension of war in Russia, heightened by Goya's grotesque and terrible visions, ultimately gave rise to his most famous poem, "I Am Goya."

After the war the family returned to Moscow. As an adolescent, Voznesensky thought of becoming an artist. Then he studied architecture. "I was already writing," he says, "but mainly I painted. Yet poetry was flowing in me like a river under the ice." Shortly before his graduation from the Moscow Architectural Institute in 1957, an event occurred which is the subject of the poem "Fire in the Architectural Institute." Like other senior students, Voznesensky had spent his last year on an elaborate design project, which he describes, with all due modesty, as "a spiral-shaped thing, a bit like the Guggenheim Museum." "One morning," he says, "we found that a fire had destroyed a year's work. Whole districts and cities on blueprints had vanished. We were so tired that we were glad that final examinations had to be postponed. But for me it was more than a fire. I believe in symbols. I understood that architecture was burned out in *me*. I became a poet."

Voznesensky's interest in painting and architecture is seen in all his poetry, most explicitly in his choice of themes and images. In "Master Craftsmen" he invokes the legend that Barma, the architect of St. Basil's Cathedral in Moscow, was blinded by Ivan the Terrible so that he might never again design anything as beautiful. Architectural images predominate in a number of his poems, such as "The Torches of Florence" and "Italian Garage." "New York Airport at Night" is one sustained metaphor of the airport as the self-portrait of the poet.

Certainly the decisive event in Voznesensky's life came soon after his abandonment of architecture. This was his meeting with Boris Pasternak. He sent his first poems to Pasternak, who replied with a letter of praise and an invitation to visit him. "From that time on I never left his side," he has said. "I moved out to Peredelkino and stayed near him till his death.... He was my only master."

Voznesensky's earliest writings are said to be derivative of Pasternak, but, judging from his first published poems (1958), he quickly found his personal and wholly original idiom. He shares, however, Pasternak's fondness for the pathetic fallacy, and his sense of the unity of all organic life is quite Pasternakian:

> I know we shall live again as
> Friends or girl friends or blades of grass,
> Instead of us this one or that one will come:
> Nature abhors a vacuum.
>
> (from "Autumn in Sigulda")

But, above all, Voznesensky bears the mark of Pasternak's moral intelligence, which has formed and armed him, as it has so many others, in the struggle to re-create a genuine literature for Russia, devastated by Stalin. In *Dr. Zhivago*, Pasternak described the enemy:

"It was then [that is, during World War I] that falsehood came into our Russian land. The great misfortune, the root of all evil to come, was the loss of faith in the value of personal opinions. People imagined that it was all out of date to follow their own moral sense, that they must all sing the same tune in chorus, and live by other people's notions, the notions which were being crammed down everybody's throat. And there arose the power of the glittering phrase, first tsarist, then revolutionary." Pasternak's celebration of individual values, his passionate insistence on the right of privacy, and his exaltation of the life of the heart provided the moral climate, above the miasma of Stalinism, in which Russian literature was revived and restored in the post-Stalin period.

Moreover, Pasternak's forty-seven years of creative work, from 1913 to 1960, bridging, as it does, the sterile years of Stalinism, have provided a point of departure from which Voznesensky and other young poets and writers have been able to proceed to their principal task: to resurrect the language which had been corrupted by the "power of the glittering phrase." Not only were such abstract nouns as "freedom," "justice," and "truth" debased, but the language of life itself was extinguished; this is perhaps one of the most terrible of the indictments contained in *Dr. Zhivago*.

It is in this context that Voznesensky's immense popularity, inconceivable in the West for a "serious" modern poet, may be fully understood. If 14,000 people congregated (as they did in 1962) in a sports stadium to hear Voznesensky read his poetry, or 100,000 subscribed to buy a book of his poetry (*The*

Triangular Pear), it is because countless Russians have ceased to attend to the "glittering phrase," turning instead to the language of symbol and fantasy for the truths they seek. One result has been the rage for poetry readings which seized Russia in the post-Stalin decade. Until the crackdown of 1963 severely curtailed poetry readings, these had become the principal entertainment of intellectuals and students in Moscow, and in provincial cities, where poets went by the truckload.

The encounter of poet and public in Russia is a moving spectacle. Voznesensky, in particular, has made of the art of recitation something like an act of communion. At first sight, however, Voznesensky's presence on stage is not overwhelming. An awkward figure, slight and singularly vulnerable, he stands before the microphone with his legs stiffly apart, his Adam's apple bobbing, bearing the applause and the shouts of acclaim as if they were blows. Then he will recite from memory for an hour or two, with hardly a pause, in a powerful, cultivated voice. His awkwardness vanishes; now it is his listeners who appear tense, straining forward to capture the flow of a language unheard of in Russia until now. Most will have brought copies of his books, which they will follow, like music scores.

Voznesensky's readings display to the fullest advantage the assonances, rhythms, and modulations of pitch and intensity which he uses with such virtuosity in composing his poems. These devices serve his intention rather as a brilliant orchestra score serves a central musical idea. ("Form isn't what counts," he says. "Form must be clear, unfathomable, disquieting, like the sky in which only radar can sense the presence of a plane.") "I Am Goya" begins: "I am Goya / of the bare field, by the enemy's beak gouged / till the craters of my eyes gape / I am grief / I am the tongue / of war, the embers of cities / on the snows of the year 1941 / I am hunger..." In Russian the assonances are devastating: *Ya Góya ... nagóye ... ya góre ... ya gólos ... góda ... ya gólod ... ya górlo ... góloi ...*

Voznesensky reads with an actor's skill. And his voice, with its amazing range of tonalities and expression, is an ideal instrument to render the changes of mood and intensity which are so characteristic of his idiom. Within the same poem, and often within the same line, he may be tender, playful, mocking, and, finally and most compellingly, ironic. He is a master of irony and to this end employs not only his technical resources (for example, punning, juxtaposing, or rhyming internally a pompous word with far-out slang) but also his alarming associations, fantasies, and images, as in "The Skull Ballad" where the severed head of Anna Mons, the mistress of Peter the Great, speaks to the Czar in these terms:

> *love is so small who cares for love*
> *in times like these men build*
> *and set a world on fire—you kiss*
> *me State in blood in blood*

When reading these lines, Voznesensky's voice, while it does not seek to imitate a woman's, is pitched, with uncanny effect, to an extremity of rage.

Here in the contrast between the slight, and rather modest, private person of Voznesensky and his commanding public presence, one glimpses the nature of his truest debt to Pasternak: a sense of the poet as prophet. "The poet is two people," Voznesensky has said. "One is an insignificant person, leading the most insignificant of lives. But behind him, like an echo, is the other person who writes poetry. Sometimes the two coexist. Sometimes they collide; this is why certain poets have had tragic ends. Often the real man has no idea what path or what action the other will take. That other man is the prophet who is in every poet. . . . When a man writes he feels his prophetic mission in the world. The task of the Russian poet today is to look deep inside man. When I read my poetry to a great number of people, their emotional, almost sensual expression of feeling seems to me to reveal the soul of man—now no longer hidden behind closed shutters, but wide open like a woman who has just been kissed."

Voznesensky's popularity has made him enemies in the literary and political establishment. The hacks who built their careers on writing odes to Stalin now feel threatened when huge printings of Voznesensky's books sell out in a single day, while their own books molder away unsold in the bookstores. The bureaucrats, whose careers and tastes were formed by Stalin, are scarcely more attuned to Voznesensky and other modern poets; their authority is undermined, they feel, when people are seen to respond with more enthusiasm to poetry than to *agit-prop*.

Conservative critics often accuse Voznesensky of "formalism" (experimentalism) and ambiguity. To the first charge he answered, in his poem "Evening on the Building Site": "They nag me about 'formalism.' / Experts, what a distance / You are from life! Formalin: / You stink of it, and incense." And again in "Antiworlds," he wrote: "Ah, my critics; how I love them. / Upon the neck of the keenest of them, / Fragrant and bald as fresh-baked bread, / There shines a perfect anti-head . . ." To the charge of ambiguity, he replied in "Who Are We?": I am myself / Among avalanches, like the Abominable / Snowman, absolutely elusive."

Criticism of Voznesensky mounted, in most menacing fashion, in 1963, during the vast official campaign against Russia's liberal-minded modernist writers and artists. The campaign was launched by Khrushchev at the now famous Manege exhibition of modern art, where he denounced the painters in a torrent of scatological abuse and equated their work with homosexuality —"and for that," he said, "you can get ten years." Khrushchev's fury turned quickly to the writers, whom he abused in much the same terms he used against the painters, at closed meetings held between government leaders and writers, artists, and other intellectuals. In its public aspect, the campaign raged for seven months in the press, and at writers' meetings held all over the country where Stalinist mediocrities proceeded to vent their pent-up anger and jealousy on nearly every young writer who had received public acclaim during the last years—particularly Voznesensky and Evtushenko. They called for an end to the editions of 100,000 copies, the favorable reviews, and the trips abroad for writers who, they claimed, flout Party opinion and play the game of Western bourgeois ideologists ("with one foot on Gorky Street and the other on Broadway") in their "rotten, overpraised, unrealistic, smelly writings."

In classic purge style, recantations were demanded of the writers. Here Voznesensky, together with most of the other writers, proved to be "absolutely elusive." Many maintained silence, or defended themselves; although the writers were hardly offered a forum in the Soviet press, reports from foreign Communist observers indicated widespread defiance at the writers' meetings. Even recantations deemed fit to print in the newspapers were often ambiguous or ironic. This was Voznesensky's response to a savage attack on him by Krushchev: "It has been said at this plenum [of the board of the Soviet Writers' Union] that I must never forget the stern and severe words of Nikita Sergeyevich [Khrushchev]. I shall never forget them. I shall not forget not only these severe words but also the advice which Nikita Sergeyevich gave me. He said: 'Work.' I do not justify myself now. I simply wish to say that for me now the main thing is to work, work, work. What my attitude is to my country, to communism, what I myself am, this work will show." (*Pravda*, March 29, 1963.)

The campaign petered out in late June of 1963. It had failed utterly in its objective to cow the writers and humiliate them before the nation, and to re-establish controls, on the Stalinist model, over literature. The writers had clearly won a moral victory. The authorities had to settle for an undeclared truce with the liberal writers which has been maintained (with some grave lapses) during the first year of the post-Khrushchev era. The writers who were under fire in 1963 gradually reappeared in print, and poetry readings were resumed, but by no means on the same scale as before.

Whatever the outcome of the campaign, the force and character of the attack on Voznesensky, and other writers, were bound to be profoundly wounding. Voznesensky was at first sent into virtual exile (it was announced that he was spending his time in factories near Vladimir), and for many months he wandered about the country:

> Beware, my darling. Hush. Not a sound,
> While I charge noisily
> From place to place around Russia,
> As a bird diverts the hunters from its nest.
> (from "My Achilles Heart")

His poems of that period are often love poems. It is love that defends and saves man from that which oppresses him:

> When trouble licked at me like flame,
> I dived into Riga, as one would into water,
> And through a straw as fair as your hair,
> You gave me your breath and your breath was air.
> (from "Oza")

Among his most affecting poems are a group suffused with the raging pain of that period. Among these are "Dead Still," "Give Me Peace," "My Achilles Heart," "The Ballad of Pain," and "The Monologue of Marilyn Monroe." (The last two poems are not included in this collection.) Most of these poems appeared, however, a year or two after the campaign against Voznesensky. His first major poem to be published after the campaign was "Longjumeau" (*Pravda*, October 13, 1963), a tribute to Lenin. Longjumeau was the Party school near Paris associated with Lenin. While the subject is, of course, eminently "acceptable," and the poet is extremely respectful of Lenin, he is by no means sycophantic. Moreover, the poem shows clearly that Voznesensky was not disposed to yield in any way to criticism of his use of language. "Longjumeau" offers splendid examples of his inventiveness in this regard: he has Lenin, while playing a Russian form of skittles (*gorodki*), throw a stick and smash "empires, / churches, future Berias" (*tak chto vdrebezgi imperii, / tserkvi, budushchie berii*). Bold and startling in its play with the grimmest of names, *imperii-berii* is also characteristic of Voznesensky's semantic exploitation of rhyme, as opposed to purely phonetic rhyming: Beria had, of course, an empire himself. Another instance of his use of this "rich" sort of rhyme was singled out by the writer Samuil Marshak in a posthumously published article (*Novy mir*, No. 9, 1965) on the work of young Russian poets. This is the rhyme *vayateli* (sculptors) and *voiteli* (warriors) in "Master Craftsmen," a poem about embattled artists. Such rhymes, besides being ingenious phonetically, reinforce the whole meaning of the poem.

In general, Voznesensky stands out among the other young poets in the Soviet Union for the resourcefulness with which he handles language. Probably none has a greater range than he. Together with Evtushenko, he has pioneered the emancipation of Russian poetic language from the restriction from which it has long suffered and given back to it something of the freedom which it enjoyed in the twenties. Where necessary for his poetic purposes, he never hesitates to introduce slang, neologisms, and the jargon of modern technology. In "Oza" he complains that his "throat is sore from technical terms." However, his use of slang and technical jargon is for the most part very disciplined. There is no question of his using this language, as lesser poets sometimes do, to flaunt his "emancipation," to indulge in the tiresome *épatage* which is all too common during the sort of poetic revolution which is going on in Russia at the moment. If he chooses an unusual word or expression, it is not for its own sake, but because he thinks it is best suited to the achievement of a particular effect. A characteristic device is his sudden, unexpected use of a slang word to bring about an abrupt change of emotional pitch. There is a good example in "Hunting a Hare": The almost unbearable tension that the hunters feel at the end of the chase, the sense of mystic awe which the death of the hare induces in them, is suddenly broken—only to be strangely heightened—by the comment of one of the hunters in the cynical language of the criminal and the police interrogator: *okhmuryaet* (roughly: "He's putting it on"). Another good example of a startling change of key in a solemn context is in "Autumn in Sigulda," where, speaking of his own tombstone, the poet uses the word *bul'dik*, which is adolescent slang for a lump of rock. Voznesensky's use of words out of their normal context can be playful and ironical in a way which does not always please his critics. A case in point is the deliberately anachronistic introduction of the term *stroitel'stvo* (literally, "construction," in Soviet political rhetoric: e.g., "the construction of communism") in his poem "The Skull Ballad," which relates to the time of Peter the Great (see the note on this poem). His rhymes, too, sometimes suggest a lack of piety which creates a feeling of unease, as it is no doubt intended to, among the strait-laced, right-minded citizens whom Voznesensky likes to tease (as in "Wall of Death," where he brackets them with Vestal Virgins). The names of venerable figures (not excluding Lenin) and awe-inspiring institutions are quite likely to be rhymed impishly with some apparently incongruous colloquialism. In "Oza," for example, the famous Soviet atomic research station in Dubna is rhymed with the slang phrase for "kicking the bucket" (*ne dam ya duba . . . Dubna*). This, needless to say, implies no disrespect for Dubna, but only disdain for pomposity and literal-mindedness. Apart from his superb mastery of contemporary Russian idiom, Voznesensky also brings to his craft an impressive knowledge of his native poetic tradition. His own original manner is enhanced by an easy familiarity with Mayakovsky and Pasternak, both of whom have influenced him, as well as with the classical Russian heritage. In "Oza" particularly there are echoes of Pushkin, Lermontov, and Blok.

His wide linguistic range is matched by the thematic variety of his work. The present collection has been subdivided into seven sections so as to group together poems which are more or less akin to each other.

Part 1: "I Am Goya" consists of work in which the poet focuses his attention on war, death, violence, and injustice. Here his vision of the world, like that of Goya, is haunted and horror-struck. Sometimes he speaks of his own anguished state (as in "My Achilles Heart"), but more generally, as in "Someone Is Beating a Woman," he is concerned with the plight of other people. In "The Skull Ballad" and "The Cashier" there is an attempt to generalize in allegorical form about the human condition. He seems to be saying that the world lies in evil and that man is a deaf-mute, like the hapless invalids in the store beating hopelessly against the glass-protected cashier's cubicle: "Drumming of knuckle and palm / On the glass plate; / So bellowed the psalm / Of my dumb fate." In "Hunting a Hare" the pursuit of a dumb animal is made into a symbol of blind and unmotivated cruelty: "The urge to kill, like the urge to beget, / Is blind and sinister . . ." Yet in all this there is no absolute despair, and sometimes even a hint of possible redemption: people can be touched or moved by the evil they see done, or even by the evil they do themselves. The poet has been criticized by some of his Soviet critics for dwelling on the "immutability" of human nature (see the note on "The Skull Ballad"), but what he rejects is only a facile and complacent belief in progress, not the idea of progress itself.

Part 2: "Give Me Peace" consists of poems of a more intimate and personal kind in which the dominant note is that of retreat, even escape, into love and nature. Some of them, as explained earlier, are closely connected with his own personal difficulties in the past few years ("Dead Still" and "Give Me Peace"), but the general sense binding all these poems together is the supreme value attached to personal relations, and the ultimate primacy of nature over history and the doings of men. If love is salvation and a refuge, to be deprived of it is the greatest misfortune and one which holds the most terror for the poet, hence the melancholy counterpoint to the comparative serenity of "Dead Still," "Bi cycles," and "Give Me Peace" in "Autumn," "First Frost," and "You sit, pregnant and pale . . ." where the miseries of loneliness, separation, and abandonment are shown in all their unrelievable bleakness.

Part 3: "Who Are We?" has as its unifying theme the problem of identifying oneself and others, the ambiguity and deceptiveness of outward appearances, the difficulty of finding one's bearings in life. "Foggy Street" gives an idea, through the appropriate image of a world shrouded in fog, of the confused notion we have even of people we think we know well. In "Who Are We?" the poet proclaims the elusiveness of his own personality, and in "Antiworlds," borrowing the concept of "anti-matter" from modern physics, he talks in a half-comic, half-serious vein of the possibility of assuming other identities or of communicating with one's "double" in the "antiworld."

Part 4: "The Parabola" is concerned with the fate and role of the artist. In "The Torches of Florence" and "Fire in the Architectural Institute," Voznesensky touches rather self-deprecatingly on some of the vicissitudes of his own career, but in most of the poems, particularly "Leaves and Roots," "Master Craftsmen," and "Parabolic Ballad," he treats more seriously of the artist's historical calling as prophet, rebel, witness, and martyr. To illustrate his theme, he ranges through several countries, mainly Russia, but also Italy and Georgia.

Part 5: "The Triangular Pear" shows the poet's preoccupation with certain aspects of the modern world, his ambivalent feelings about its technology and its hectic tempo, which both enthrall and disturb him. Most of this group of poems were written under the influence of the impressions he gained during his journey to America in 1961.

Part 6: "I'm a Family of Seven" is a miscellany of poems in a lighter vein, sometimes humorous, or whimsical.

Part 7: "Oza" is the poet's most ambitious work, in which he attempts to give a more elaborate statement of his view of the world. Despite the bewildering complexity of the poem's structure, its alternation of prose and verse, and its abrupt changes in mood ranging from the lyrical to the satirical (with elements of mystification and parody), the work nonetheless has certain unifying threads. One is the chronicle of an ill-starred secret love affair. Never wholly abandoning this crucial personal theme, the poet moves from time to time to a speculative plane, expressing ideas on the state of the world in general, the history of his country, and man's condition. He is at once fascinated and repelled by modern technology, which is personified by the cyclotron and its master (who appears as the Scientist or the Toastmaster). On this theme, the poem in Section XII is most explicit: "All progress is retrogression / If the process breaks man down." In "Oza," as in many of his other poems, Voznesensky is engaged in a defense of love and of the free human spirit against "pseudo-progress" and the "god-damned machine," which, when it gets into the hands of the soul-less and heartless, begets oppression. Here, it is the poet who comes forward as the essential guardian of human values.

The translation of Voznesensky's work presents the usual difficulties of interpreting the whole complex of cultural references, even of everyday sights and sounds, a knowledge of which the poet takes for granted in his native audience, but which are unfamiliar or at best exotic to an audience rooted in a different tradition. It would be unrealistic not to admit that all translation, particularly of poetry, is to a certain extent doomed to failure, except when it deals with the abstractions of science or the international commonplaces of journalism. The peculiar flavor of the original can never, of course, be rendered, but meaning and imagery, if not the wealth of associations and allusions of the original, can survive the crashing of the language barrier. This collection, apart from being an attempt to present the work of a young Russian poet who speaks with particular urgency to the world at large, is something of an experiment in verse translation. The six American poets who contributed to this volume made their versions in close collaboration with Max Hayward. They have tried to convey, in the terms of their own poetic idiom and vision, the essence of what Voznesensky says in Russian to his compatriots.

The Editors

ACKNOWLEDGMENTS

This work was made possible by the generous grants of the Humanities Fund and the Overbrook Foundation. Miss Blake wishes to express her thanks for the support of the Russian Institute of Columbia University, where she was a Research Associate during the period in which she worked on this book. The editors owe a special debt of gratitude to Professor Philip E. Mosely, whose enthusiasm for this enterprise was a constant source of encouragement.

Contents

1

I AM GOYA

I AM GOYA

I am Goya
of the bare field, by the enemy's beak gouged
till the craters of my eyes gape
I am grief

I am the tongue
of war, the embers of cities
on the snows of the year 1941
I am hunger

I am the gullet
of a woman hanged whose body like a bell
tolled over a blank square
I am Goya

O grapes of wrath!
I have hurled westward
     the ashes of the uninvited guest!
and hammered stars into the unforgetting sky—like nails
I am Goya

TRANSLATED BY STANLEY KUNITZ

MY ACHILLES HEART

In these days of unheard-of suffering
One is lucky indeed to have no heart:
Crack shots plug me again and again,
But have no luck.

Riddled with holes, I laugh
At the furious pack: "Tallyho, boys!
I am a lattice. Look through me.
Isn't the landscape lovely?"

But suppose a gun should locate,
Tied by an aching thread,
Beating a hairbreadth off target,
My Achilles heart.

Beware, my darling. Hush. Not a sound,
While I charge noisily
From place to place around Russia,
As a bird diverts the hunters from its nest.

Are you still in pain? Do you act up at night?
This defenseless extra is what saves me.
Do not handle it roughly;
The shudder would bring me down.

Our destruction is unthinkable,
More unthinkable what we endure,
More unthinkable still that a sniper
Should ever sever the quivering thread.

TRANSLATED BY W. H. AUDEN

WALL OF DEATH   *to N. Androsova*

Casting her spell and daring death,
A woman zooms round the wall of death!
With leather leggings
                    as red as crabs' claws,
And wicked red lips that give one pause,
She hurtles—horizontal torpedo—
A chrysanthemum stuck in her belt.

Atomic angel, Amazon,
With cratered cheeks in-drawn,
Your motorcycle passes overhead,
Its noise, a power saw's.

Living vertically is such a bore,
Darling barbarian, daughter of Icarus . . .
It's the plight
Only of vestal virgin and suburbanite
To live vertical and upright.

In this creature who soars
Over awnings, ovations, posters, and jeers
I now can see
                    the horizontal essence of woman
Float before me!

Ah, how her orbit whirls her round the wall,
Her tears nailed to each eyeball;
And her trainer, Singichants,
Bullies her like Genghis Khan . . .

Says Singichants: "Let me tell you I
Have my hands full with that one, plastered up there like a fly!
And yesterday she had a flat . . . the little schemer . . . ! 'I'll write
                    to the boss,' says she;
And claws at my face like a mad gypsy."

During intermission I make my way
To her . . . "Instruct me in the horizontal!" I say.

5

But she stands there like lead,
The Amazon, and shakes her head;
Still shaking, dizzy from the wall,
Her eyes blurred with
                    such longing
                              for the horizontal!

TRANSLATED BY WILLIAM JAY SMITH

HUNTING A HARE   *to my friend Yuri*

Hunting a hare. Our dogs are raising a racket;
Racing, barking, eager to kill, they go,
And each of us in a yellow jacket
Like oranges against the snow.

One for the road. Then, off to hound a hare,
My cab driver friend who hates a cop, I,
Buggins' brother and his boy, away we tear.
Our jalopy,

That technological marvel, goes bounding,
Scuttling along on its snow chains. Tallyho!
After a hare we go.
Or is it ourselves we're hounding?

I'm all dressed up for the chase
In boots and jacket: the snow is ablaze.
But why, Yuri, why,
Do my gun sights dance? Something is wrong, I know,
When a glassful of living blood has to fly
In terror across the snow.

The urge to kill, like the urge to beget,
Is blind and sinister. Its craving is set
Today on the flesh of a hare: tomorrow it can
Howl the same way for the flesh of a man.

Out in the open the hare
Lay quivering there
Like the gray heart of an immense
Forest or the heart of silence:

Lay there, still breathing,
Its blue flanks heaving,
Its tormented eye a woe,
Blinking there on the cheek of the snow.

Then, suddenly, it got up,
Stood upright: suddenly,

Over the forest, over the dark river,
The air was shivered
By a human cry,

Pure, ultrasonic, wild,
Like the cry of a child.
I knew that hares moan, but not like this:
This was the note of life, the wail
Of a woman in travail,

The cry of leafless copses
And bushes hitherto dumb,
The unearthly cry of a life
Which death was about to succumb,

Nature is all wonder, all silence:
Forest and lake and field and hill
Are permitted to listen and feel,
But denied utterance.

Alpha and Omega, the first and the last
Word of Life as it ebbs away fast,
As, escaping the snare, it flies
Up to the skies.

For a second only, but while
It lasted we were turned to stone
Like actors in a movie-still.

The boot of the running cab driver hung in mid-air,
And four black pellets halted, it seemed,
Just short of their target:
Above the horizontal muscles,
The blood-clotted fur of the neck,
A face flashed out.

With slanting eyes set wide apart, a face
As in frescoes of Dionysus,
Staring at us in astonishment and anger,
It hovered there, made one with its cry,
Suspended in space,

The contorted transfigured face
Of an angel or a singer.

Like a long-legged archangel a golden mist
Swam through the forest.
"Shit!" spat the cab driver. "The little faking freak!":
A tear rolled down on the boy's cheek.

Late at night we returned,
The wind scouring our faces: they burned
Like traffic lights as, without remark,
We hurtled through the dark.

TRANSLATED BY W. H. AUDEN

THE SKULL BALLAD
A Digression into the Seventeenth Century

The peasants flock from miles around
To gape at the terrible Czar
And jeer and spit at his spying bitch,
That dirty foreigner.

The Czar is skinny as a nag
And black as anthracite;
His eyes slide over his coal-black face
Like a skidding motorbike.

Her head rolls from the blow of his axe
To the toe of his hunter's boot;
He dangles it high above the crowd
Like a red-topped turnip root.

He grips her cheeks in an iron vise,
He cracks the bridge of her nose;
The blood spurts from her golden throat
On her executioner's clothes.

He kisses her full upon the mouth,
While a groan sweeps through the crowd,
And suddenly silence stuns the square
As the death's-head speaks aloud:

"beloved one O worshipful Czar
I will not judge thy guilt
but why do thy hands stick to my skin
and taste of my own heart's salt

let me confess my womanhood
my crime deserves the whip
I tremble where that crimson fleck
hangs on thy bristling lip

love is so small who cares for love
in times like these men build

and set a world on fire—you kiss
me State in blood in blood

what if you reek of borscht and peas
such passion has a flavor
Progress you drive me mad for you
I want you to rule forever"

Stockstill the greatest of the Czars
Stood black as blackest bread;
A witness from abroad jerked back
Like a spike rammed to its head.

TRANSLATED BY STANLEY KUNITZ

SOMEONE IS BEATING A WOMAN

Someone is beating a woman.
In the car that is dark and hot
Only the whites of her eyes shine.
Her legs thrash against the roof
Like berserk searchlight beams.

Someone is beating a woman.
This is the way slaves are beaten.
Frantic, she wrenches open the door
And plunges out—onto the road.

Brakes scream.
Someone runs up to her,
Strikes her and drags her, face down,
In the grass lashing with nettles.

Scum, how meticulously he beats her,
Stilyaga, bastard, big hero,
His smart flatiron-pointed shoe
Stabbing into her ribs.

Such are the pleasures of enemy soldiers
And the brute refinements of peasants.
Trampling underfoot the moonlit grass,
Someone is beating a woman.

Someone is beating a woman.
Century on century, no end to this.
It's the young that are beaten. Somberly
Our wedding bells start up the alarum.
Someone is beating a woman.

What about the flaming weals
In the braziers of their cheeks?
That's life, you say. Are you telling me?
Someone is beating a woman.

But her light is unfaltering
World-without-ending.
There are no religions,
                            no revelations,
There are women.

Lying there pale as water
Her eyes tear-closed and still,
She doesn't belong to him
Any more than a meadow deep in a wood.

And the stars? Rattling in the sky
Like raindrops against black glass,
Plunging down,
                    they cool
Her grief-fevered forehead.

TRANSLATED BY JEAN GARRIGUE

THE CASHIER

The dumb herd scowled:
"You've short-changed us," they howled.
Pennies like medals stuck in the crust
Of sawdust.

The cashier flew into a rage—
"Nonsense! Be off with you! Go!"—
And rose like dough
From her glass cage.

Over counters where they sell
Cheesecakes and melons was blown
A sudden smell
Of tears and ozone.

Loud was the smell of tears
Among that lowing crowd:
The hands of one dumb pair
Howled in the air.

Clutching bacon, somebody swore,
Or so I imagined: at least, he
Gave a Beethovenish roar,
Earthy and shaggy.

Drumming of knuckle and palm
On the glass plate;
So bellowed the psalm
Of my dumb fate.

With a knowing leer
The cashier
Peered at a bill she held up to the light
To see if Lenin's profile looked all right.

But Lenin wasn't there any more:
The bill was counterfeit.
It was a grocery store
Where people and farces meet.

TRANSLATED BY W. H. AUDEN

2

GIVE ME PEACE

AUTUMN IN SIGULDA

Hanging out of the train, I
Bid you all goodbye.

Goodbye, Summer:
My time is up.
Axes knock at the *dacha*
As they board it up:
Goodbye.

The woods have shed their leaves,
Empty and sad today
As an accordion case that grieves
When its music is taken away.

People (meaning us)
Are also empty,
As we leave behind
(We have no choice)
Walls, mothers, womankind:
So it has always been and will be.

Goodbye, Mother,
Standing at the window
Transparent as a cocoon: soon
You will know how tired you are.
Let us sit here a bit.

Friends and foes, adieu,
Goodbye.
The whistle has blown: it is time
For you to run out of me and I
Out of you.

Motherland, goodbye now.
I shall not whimper nor make a scene,
But be a star, a willow:
Thank you, Life, for having been.

In the shooting gallery
Where the top score is ten,
I tried to reach a century:
Thank you for letting me make the mistake,
But a triple thank-you that into

My transparent shoulders
Genius drove
Like a red male fist that enters
A rubber glove.

Voznesensky may one day be graven
In cold stone but, meanwhile, may
I find haven
On your warm cheek as *Andrei*.

In the woods the leaves were already falling
When you ran into me, asked me something.
Your dog was with you: you tugged at his leash and called him,
He tugged the other way:
Thank you for that day.

I came alive: thank you for that September,
For explaining me to myself. The housekeeper, I remember,
Woke us at eight, and on weekends her phonograph sang
Some old underworld song
In a hoarse bass:
I give thanks for the time, the place.

But you are leaving, going
As the train is going, leaving,
Going in another direction: we are ceasing to belong
To each other or this house. What is wrong?

Near to me, I say:
Yet Siberias away!

I know we shall live again as
Friends or girl friends or blades of grass,
Instead of us this one or that one will come:
Nature abhors a vacuum.

The leaves are swept away without trace
But millions more will grow in their place:
Thank you, Nature, for the laws you gave me.

But a woman runs down the track
Like a red autumn leaf at the train's back.

Save me!

TRANSLATED BY W. H. AUDEN

DEAD STILL

Now, with your palms on the blades of my shoulders,
Let us embrace:
Let there be only your lips' breath on my face,
Only, behind our backs, the plunge of rollers.

Our backs, which like two shells in moonlight shine,
Are shut behind us now;
We lie here huddled, listening brow to brow,
Like life's twin formula or double sign.

In folly's world-wide wind
Our shoulders shield from the weather
The calm we now beget together,
Like a flame held between hand and hand.

Does each cell have a soul within it?
If so, fling open all your little doors,
And all your souls shall flutter like the linnet
In the cages of my pores.

Nothing is hidden that shall not be known.
Yet by no storm of scorn shall we
Be pried from this embrace, and left alone
Like muted shells forgetful of the sea.

Meanwhile, O load of stress and bother,
Lie on the shells of our backs in a great heap:
It will but press us closer, one to the other.

We are asleep.

TRANSLATED BY RICHARD WILBUR

FIRST FROST

A girl is freezing in a telephone booth,
huddled in her flimsy coat,
her face stained by tears
and smeared with lipstick.

She breathes on her thin little fingers.
Fingers like ice. Glass beads in her ears.

She has to beat her way back alone
down the icy street.

First frost. A beginning of losses.
The first frost of telephone phrases.

It is the start of winter glittering on her cheek,
the first frost of having been hurt.

TRANSLATED BY STANLEY KUNITZ

AUTUMN

The flapping of ducks' wings.
And on the pathways in the parks
the shimmer of the last cobwebs
and of the last bicycle spokes.

You should listen to what they are hinting:
go knock at the door of the last house for leavetaking;
in that proper house a woman lives
who does not expect a husband for supper.

She will release the bolt for me
and nuzzle against my coat,
she will laugh as she offers her lips to me;
and suddenly, gone limp, she will understand everything—
the autumn call of the fields,
the scattering of seed in the wind, the breakup of families. . .

Still young, trembling with cold,
she will think about how
even the apple tree bears fruit
and the old brown cow has a calf

and how life ferments in the hollows of oaks,
in pastures, in houses, in windswept woods,
ripening with the grain, treading with woodcocks,
and she will weep, sick with desire,

whispering, "What good are they to me:
my hands, my breasts? What sense does it make
to live as I do, lighting the stove,
repeating my daily round of work?"

And I shall embrace her—
I who can't make sense of it either—
while outside, in the first hoarfrost,

the fields turn aluminum.
Across them—black across them—black and gray
my footprints will march
to the railway station.

TRANSLATED BY STANLEY KUNITZ

THE PARTY

All the tipsy crew
Sat down. Suddenly. . . .
Where are they?
                Those two?
Gone!
      Not there!

Were they blown away by the wind
At the height of the fun, leaving behind
A pair of empty chairs,
Two knives lying there?

A moment ago they were drinking.
They were here. In a twinkling
They vanished, banished from view,
Away, those two.

Off through the slush they ran—
Catch-them-if-you-can!—
They have burned their boats.
To hell with conventions and raincoats!

So from the wineglass fades the hum
When the finger ceases to strum,
So races a river down its bed,
Or a cloud overhead.

So youth is bold to flout
The old and their apron strings,
So in spring young saplings
Break out.

The party is a huge success:
But the daring of this pair,
The back of each deserted chair,
Leave one speechless.

TRANSLATED BY W. H. AUDEN

You sit, pregnant and pale.
How you are changed, poor girl!

You sit pulling at your skirt
As you start to cry and cry . . .

No wonder we are spoiled!
Women, abandoned, fall to our lips,

Dash out at the crossing
When the train chugs off,

And stumble along the tracks,
Like you, staring at window streaks.

Mail trains, express trains rattle past
To nearby towns or vast Siberia . . .

And from Moscow to Ashkhabad,
Numbed and dumbstruck,

Women like monoliths stand,
Showing their bellies to the moon;

While the great-bellied earth,
Trapped in the bleak enormity of space,

As it spins to the light,
Interprets them.

BICYCLES   *to V. Bokov*

In the wood, in the dew
Bicycles lie.
Through birch-trunk gaps
The road flashes by.

Fender to fender,
Fallen they are;
Pedal to pedal,
Handlebar to handlebar.

Try as you will,
No voice can attain
These torpid monsters
Tangled in chain.

Vacant and huge,
Upward they gaze;
Above—green mist
Of resin and bees.

In mint and daisies
Rippling deep,
Forgotten they lie,
And sleep, sleep.

TRANSLATED BY WILLIAM JAY SMITH

HOMELESS

We're hoboes,
          hoboes traveling light,
lucky to borrow
          a bed for the night,
careless about tomorrow.

Spiritualists
          might steal here for their trysts;
this hideout has more echoes than a church,
it's full of other people's lives;
the place rocks
          with chromos and priests . . .
Come on!
          let's raid the icebox.

Not for us the song of the gas stove,
let the telephone ring—it's not for us.

We're closest, aren't we, when we're most away,
embraced
          by ghostly strangers in the dark,
whose kisses scald and stay.

My dearest, what a sorry tune!
We're émigrés on foreign soil,
condemned in a cold and heartless town
to hide the deepest things we feel.

Shame on fat-bellied bureaucrats!
but what's the scandal, what's the crime
that we should keep each other warm?
The orators tell dirty lies,
but whom, I ask, do we two harm?
Shopkeepers, why are you disturbed by us?
Fear for yourselves, who think love dangerous.

Dreary cellars of our buried life!
Shall we burn up the wallpaper when we wake?
            attack the pictures with a knife?
smash every piece of china into bits
            for love's departing sake?
"Be careful with that dish, it isn't ours to break."

TRANSLATED BY STANLEY KUNITZ

GIVE ME PEACE

Give me quietness and peace . . .
My nerves are badly burnt, I guess,
give me peace . . .

           Let the pine tree slowly shift
its shadow which tickles us as it goes
down our backs all the way to our toes
with a kind of cooling mischief.
Give us peace . . .

All sounds have ceased.
Why put in words the iridescence
of your eyebrows? You nod in silence.
Give us peace.

Sound travels much slower
than light: let's give our tongues a rest
—in any case, essentials are nameless,
better rely on feeling and color.

The skin is also human, dear,
with sensations peculiar to it:
a finger's touch is music to it,
like a nightingale's song to the ear.

What's with you windbags back at home?
Still shouting blue murder and fussing?
Still raising hell about nothing?
Leave us alone . . .

. . . we're deep in something else,
immersed in nature's inscrutable ways.
From an acrid smell of smoke we surmise
that the shepherds are back from the hills.

It's dusk. They're cooking their suppers
and smoking, each as hushed as his shadow,
and like flames of cigarette lighters
the silent tongues of sheep dogs glow.

TRANSLATED BY MAX HAYWARD

31

3

WHO ARE WE?

FOGGY STREET

The air is gray-white as a pigeon feather.
          Police bob up like corks on a fishing net.
Foggy weather.
What century is it? What era? I forget.

As in a nightmare, everything is crumbling;
          people have come unsoldered; nothing's intact . . .
I plod on, stumbling—
Or flounder in cotton wool, to be more exact.

Noses. Parking lights. Badges flash and blur.
          All's vague, as at a magic-lantern show.
Your hat check, sir?
Mustn't walk off with the wrong head, you know.

It's as if a woman who's scarcely left your lips
          should blur in the mind, yet trouble it with recall—
Bereft now, widowed by your love's eclipse—
          still yours, yet suddenly not yours at all . . .

Can that be Venus? No—an ice-cream vendor!
          I bump into curbstones, bump into passers-by . . .
Are they friends, I wonder?
Home-bred Iagos, how covert you are, how sly!

Why, it's you, my darling, shivering there alone!
          Your overcoat's too big for you, my dear.
But why have you grown
That mustache? Why is there frost in your hairy ear!

I trip. I stagger. I persist.
          Murk, murk . . . there's nothing visible anywhere.
Whose is the cheek you brush now in the mist?
Ahoy there!
One's voice won't carry in this heavy air . . .

When the fog lifts, how brilliant it is, how rare!

TRANSLATED BY RICHARD WILBUR

35

THE LAST TRAIN TO MALAKHOVKA

Boys with fancy flick knives,
Girls with brassy gold-crowned smiles,
Two conductresses, those stony
Sphinxes, cat-napping . . .

They're all nodding, our workaday citizens,
The coach is blacked out with sleep
Except at the end of the car where jigs
A hubbub of drunken strings.

I'm there too, near the door,
To get away from the heat and snores.
Around me throbbing like a gypsy camp
Thieves and guitars . . .

I happen to start to say a poem
To some of these toughs in the shadows . . .
Cigarette butts, a litter of
Spat-out sunflower seeds . . .

They've rackets of their own
But I recite to them
About a girl who's crying
In the glassy night of a telephone booth.

They've been up before the judge a hundred times
They don't care what happens to them
They've got away with murder
And figure that they always can

You think they give a damn about that girl
Crying in the telephone booth?
For them she's no more than this one here
All bangs, plastered with powder.

. . . You stand there, you've got
That soggy used-up look,
Your blouse records the fingerprints
Of half the boys in Malakhovka,

Yet it's you who are crying stormily
And shining with tears
Whisper to me obscenely
The purest words

And then from the train
Astounding everyone
You leap to the platform—
Purer than Beatrice.

TRANSLATED BY JEAN GARRIGUE

STRIPTEASE

Playing her crazy part,
                         the dancer begins to take all
Her clothes off. . . . Do I bawl
Or is it the lights that make my eyes smart?

She rips off a scarf, a shawl, her tinsel and fringe,
As one would slowly peel an orange.

Her eyes like a bird's are haunted with miseries
As she does her striptease.

It's terrifying. In the bar, wolf calls, bald pates.
Like leeches with blood
The drunkards' eyes inflate.

That redhead, like someone bespattered with egg yolk,
Is transformed into a pneumatic drill!
The other, a bedbug,
                      is horrible and apoplectic;
And the saxophone howls on, apocalyptic.

Universe, I curse your lack of edges,
And the Martian lights on your sweeping bridges;
I curse you,
                adoring and marveling, as
This downpour of woman responds to jazz.

"Are you America?" I'll ask like an idiot;
She'll sit down, tap her cigarette.

"Are you kidding, kiddo?" she'll answer me.
"Better make mine a double martini!"

TRANSLATED BY WILLIAM JAY SMITH

TRIPTYCH

I'm banished into myself
                              I'm Mikhailovskoye
my three pine trees shine and intertwine

in the murky mirror of my face
elks and pergolas grow dim at dusk

the river and I are the universe
and from some other place outside us

three red suns are blazing
three trees like glass are shivering

like a set of three *matroshkas*
three women shimmer one inside the other

one loves me and shakes with laughter
in her another flutters like a cage bird

crimson as a red-hot coal the third
crouches sullen in the center

this one will never forgive me
this one will take her revenge on me

her face is glinting at me there
like a ring from the bottom of a well

TRANSLATED BY MAX HAYWARD

ANTIWORLDS

The clerk Bukashkin is our neighbor.
His face is gray as blotting paper.

But like balloons of blue or red,
Bright Antiworlds
                float over his head!
On them reposes, prestidigitous,
Ruling the cosmos, a demon-magician,
Anti-Bukashkin the Academician,
Lapped in the arms of Lollobrigidas.

But Anti-Bukashkin's dreams are the color
Of blotting paper, and couldn't be duller.

Long live Antiworlds! They rebut
With dreams the rat race and the rut.
For some to be clever, some must be boring.
No deserts? No oases, then.

There are no women—
              just anti-men.
In the forests, anti-machines are roaring.
There's the dirt of the earth, as well as the salt.
If the earth broke down, the sun would halt.

Ah, my critics; how I love them.
Upon the neck of the keenest of them,
Fragrant and bald as fresh-baked bread,
There shines a perfect anti-head . . .

. . . I sleep with windows open wide;
Somewhere a falling star invites,
And skyscrapers
              like stalactites
Hang from the planet's underside.
There, upside down,
                  below me far,
Stuck like a fork into the earth,

Or perching like a carefree moth,
My little Antiworld,
                    there you are!

In the middle of the night, why is it
That Antiworlds are moved to visit?

Why do they sit together, gawking
At the television, and never talking?

Between them, not one word has passed.
Their first strange meeting is their last.

Neither can manage the least *bon ton.*
Oh, how they'll blush for it, later on!

Their ears are burning like a pair
Of crimson butterflies, hovering there . . .

. . . A distinguished lecturer lately told me,
"Antiworlds are a total loss."

Still, my apartment-cell won't hold me.
I thrash in my sleep, I turn and toss.

And, radio-like, my cat lies curled
With his green eye tuned in to the world.

TRANSLATED BY RICHARD WILBUR

GEORGIAN ROADS

Your shoulders were gripped
by the paws of epaulets,
but you tore free and risked
your necks—hussars and poets!

Your pelisses and tunics
raced past tortoises of hills
and the regimental medics
rummaged in your skulls,

but your songs live on,
like the ring of horseshoes
they soared up to heaven
and echoed back to us.

Some Georgian highway
hurled them in its catapult
to land them at our doorway
with the whine of a cannonball.

Now once again, looping
the loop on these same routes,
new daredevils are hooting:
truck drivers and poets!

Their headlights dart
and spiral skywards.
For God's sake have a heart!
Where are you taking us?

Through the mountain air,
into far reaches of future ages
these poets and truck drivers blare
their lofty wind-borne messages.

TRANSLATED BY MAX HAYWARD

MARCHÉ AUX PUCES

1

Sell me, Fleamarket,
I dote on your triste keepsakes.   .
It's a cross between old blues and a barcarolle
Your candelabra, samovars—
Menagerie of dusty things!
Their pent-up centuries cry in you
Like elephants who trumpet for
Their rainy forests—freedom, youth—
In aging zoos.

Rings, rusty bagatelles,
What breasts gleamed in you?

Here's armor, like a cast-off shell,
And whose was this cartouche?
Broken horseheads! Mustangs! Pinchbeck skulls!
If things had souls you'd be their fingerprints!
Temple of junk, Fleamarket!
Your clutter makes a small lost tune
My Muse waltzes to.

Loveseat, your springs gushed out,
Where are your lolling girls?

Can an hourglass measure centuries?
This fine suede, worn at the fingertips,
Coquetted with whose cheeks?

Love! What's its price today, and poetry
Of the useless, utilitarian kind?

How much near-madness, shyness?
What's the good of metaphors to robots?

Sell me, little cast-offs,
I'm obsolete as you!
When Robot Ten comes off the line
There's no use for One or Nine.

My sadness, Fleamarket,
Is possessive as ivy
Or time's green tinge that works its stealth
On cuirasses and leather.
A nail juts up through plush—
Scrap iron! Scrap iron!
As in Picasso's sculpture studio.

I remember him in toreador trousers
Knotting things into centuries
His eye spinning like a ball bearing
Right at his temple, his temple.
(He is a Spaniard and a walking wound.
Once a message came from Franco.
Picasso answered: His portrait? Sure.
Just send me his head!)

I read my poems to him, trembling . . .
Their echoes boomeranged
Until those figures from his canvases
Slunk into the corridors.
Age of fallout shelters, caves!
These diagrams of our anatomies
Make us vertical and askew—
Like hourglasses!

Snow sifts down on oranges,
Summered beaches,
Figures pygmied on mountains.
We're unnumbered as the sands
And sad as grains of sand
Driven down those devil
Traps of narrow-waisting hourglasses.
Don't beef! It's history we're in
For a particle of time.
We're grains of sand? But sand that can spike
And explode cannon barrels
To hell and back.

3

Fleamarket, Fleamarket,
I'm shouting, but who hears?
Your things are stormed and gray
                    as after an atomic war.
I am your *thing*, Twentieth Century.
Suppose they say to me: "You're through!"
What if my rhythms are passé.
Let the youngest moderns sneer.
Poetry won't die.

What if a crudely programmed
Archangel
                made of nuts and bolts
Rasps to me: "You're through!"
Then, Fleamarket, take me in,
I'll slip into a corner like an out-of-fashion jacket.
I'm obsolete!
                    —like a rocket-launching pad
Excavated in the desert!

TRANSLATED BY JEAN GARRIGUE

WHO ARE WE?

Who are we? Ciphers or great men?
There is no physicist no lyricist blood.
Genius is in the planet's blood.
You're either a poet or a Lilliputian.

We are inoculated
Against time, with time—whatever we are.
"What are you?" jolts and spins the head
Like a race car.

Who are you? Suppose you're something wrong,
A plaster cast of Venus in a raincoat,
A starling with a rooster's song,
An architect turned into a poet.

What are you? Mooning to be a film star,
Out of school you cut off your long hair,
Become a salesgirl in a shop,
And within a few weeks give it up.

As if playing hide-and-seek
You walk into half-world streets of Moscow,
A little fawn in heat, you stop and peek,
Out of breath, on your own.

Walking along. Who are you?
You look into bookshop windows and men's eyes,
A toy telescope you scan the skies
Of their motionless pupils. Who are you?

Under the cold stars, I wander alive
With you Vera, Vega, I am myself
Among avalanches, like the Abominable
Snowman, absolutely elusive.

TRANSLATED BY STANLEY MOSS

46

4

THE PARABOLA

PARABOLIC BALLAD

Along a parabola life like a rocket flies,
Mainly in darkness, now and then on a rainbow.
Red-headed bohemian Gauguin the painter
Started out life as a prosperous stockbroker.
In order to get to the Louvre from Montmartre
He made a detour all through Java, Sumatra,
Tahiti, the Isles of Marquesas.
                                With levity
He took off in flight from the madness of money,
The cackle of women, the frowst of academies,
Overpowered the force of terrestrial gravity.
The high priests drank their porter and kept up their jabbering:
"Straight lines are shorter, less steep than parabolas.
It's more proper to copy the heavenly mansions."

He rose like a howling rocket, insulting them
With a gale that tore off the tails of their frock coats.
So he didn't steal into the Louvre by the front door
But on a parabola smashed through the ceiling.
In finding their truths lives vary in daring:
Worms come through holes and bold men on parabolas.

There once was a girl who lived in my neighborhood.
We went to one school, took exams simultaneously.
But I took off with a bang,
                                I went whizzing
Through the prosperous double-faced stars of Tiflis.
Forgive me for this idiotic parabola.
Cold shoulders in a pitch-dark vestibule . . .
Rigid, erect as a radio antenna rod
Sending its call sign out through the freezing
Dark of the universe, how you rang out to me,
An undoubtable signal, an earthly stand-by
From whom I might get my flight bearings to land by.
The parabola doesn't come to us easily.

Laughing at law with its warnings and paragraphs
Art, love, and history race along recklessly
Over a parabolic trajectory.

He is leaving tonight for Siberia.
                              Perhaps
A straight line after all is the shorter one actually.

TRANSLATED BY W. H. AUDEN

BALLAD OF 1941

The piano has crawled underground. Hauled
In for firewood, sprawled
With frozen barrels, crates, and sticks,
The piano is waiting for the axe.

Legless, a black box,
It lies on its belly like a lizard,
Droning, heaving, backed
In an empty mine shaft.

Blood-red, his frozen fingers swollen,
Three lost on one hand, he goes down
On his hands and knees
To reach the keys.

Seven fingers of an ex-pianist play,
Their frost-bitten skin, steaming, peels away
As from a boiled potato. Their beauty,
Their godliness flame and reply,

Like the great northern lights.
Everything played before is a great lie.
All the reflections of flaming chandeliers,
The white columns, the grand tiers

In warm concert halls—a great lie.
But the steel of the piano howls in me.
I lie in that catacomb,
And I am huge as that piano.

I mirror the soot of the mine. I ape
Hunger, the light of fires, the human shape.
And for my crowning crescendo
I wait for the lick of the axe.

TRANSLATED BY STANLEY MOSS

LEAVES AND ROOTS

They carried him not to bury him:
They carried him down to crown him.

Grayer than granite,
More reddish than bronze,
Steaming like a locomotive,
The poet flourished here,
                              disheveled,
Who would not bow before votive lamps
But to the common spade.

The lilac at his doorstep burned . . .
A fountain of falling stars
                              soaked in sweat,
His back steamed
Like a loaf in the oven.

Now his house gapes, vacant,
Tenantless;
There is nobody in the dining room,
There is not a soul in Russia.

It is the way of the poet to search
For sanctuary. He goes hatless,
                    as people do in church,
Through the murmuring fields
To the birch grove and the oaks.

In his flight is his victory;
In his retreat, an ascent
To pastures and planets
Far from lying ornament.

Forests shed their crowns of leaves,
But powerfully underground
Roots twist and thrust
Like a gnarled hand.

TRANSLATED BY STANLEY KUNITZ

MASTER CRAFTSMEN

(First Dedication)

Minstrels play, bells
peal and chime

for you,
artists
of all times,

for you,
Michelangelo,
Barma, Dante
burnt alive by the lightning
of your own
incandescent talent.

Your chisels, as they hewed
statue or pillar,
could knock a crown off its head
and shake the seats of power.

For an artist true-born
revolt is second nature:
he is both tribune
and troublemaker.

They've bricked you up in walls
and burned you at the stake,
and the priests like swarms
of ants have danced at your wake.

But art survives
the hangman and the rack
to spark, like flint,
against the stones of Moabit.

In sweat and ashes,
bloody and callused,

like Zoya,
          the Muses
go to the gallows,

but against their holy writ
there is no recipe,
to all who fight with a sculptor's mallet
glory be!

(Second Dedication)

Moscow seethes like broth,
bells rage

at you,
barbarians
of every age!

Tyrants and Czars
in blazing regalia,
oval tiaras
and cannon-shaped top hats,

your moneybags and empire
insuring against fire,
in Pegasus you saw
nothing but a Trojan horse!

You dread the artist's hand
and Barma's burnt-out eyes
glowing
like brands
at dead of night.

By my words you are condemned
and branded,
may you be
forever damned!

TRANSLATED BY MAX HAYWARD

54

THE TORCHES OF FLORENCE

Florence, phosphorescent, looms,
Opening, like a guardian who twists
Keys in the locks of ancient rooms,
Its palazzos and its heavy mists.

The palazzos I know. I had no aversion
To aping—for bathhouses—their detail;
The Baptistery's a slightly better version
Of my blueprint for a local jail.

Socialist Realism's offspring wafted,
Wayward, to these lamplit squares,
Florence, plan that my youth drafted,
Past great façades, through giant doors

I wander on into my past;
Through tracing paper there appears,
In full outline, the Moscow cast
Of comrades launched on their careers.

Here at my back they all are bending,
Goggle-eyed at my interviews,
Angels, flunkies, here attending,
Drinking in my latest news.

The lamps above the Arno's black
Are somewhat more than I can stand,
Like automobiles wheeling back,
Sidelights blazing on each hand.

"Hey, you—architect!" my vows indict
Me now, along with my drawing board,
Matches, cigarettes piled up at night.
"You there!" the palazzos roar
As they come crowding in.
"The young should not be paid in advance,
You bad boy."

Among them stands, with vacant look,
A fellow, new to the platform, whose
Face is the blank page of a notebook,
String dangling from his gaping shoes.

"You're way out in front," says he, "right?
Behaving properly, doing well?
Salesgirls know you now by sight;
Even abroad your poems sell.

Then why just now did I see you crying?
To whom do the torches say farewell—
There above the palazzos flying,
So fresh and so funereal?"

I've a 10:30 date. I cut him off.
The reporters are waiting—I must be off.

I climb into my car. The doors are wet;
Backward-speeding, Florence sways.
Card castles with bright hearts inset,
Torch-studded, the palazzos blaze.

TRANSLATED BY WILLIAM JAY SMITH

FIRE IN THE ARCHITECTURAL INSTITUTE

Fire in the Architectural Institute!
through all the rooms and over the blueprints
like an amnesty through the jails . . .
Fire! Fire!

High on the sleepy façade
shamelessly, mischievously
like a red-assed baboon
a window skitters.

We'd already written our theses,
the time had come for us to defend them.
They're crackling away in a sealed cupboard:
all those bad reports on me!

The drafting paper is wounded,
it's a red fall of leaves;
my drawing boards are burning,
whole cities are burning.

Five summers and five winters shoot up in flames
like a jar of kerosene.
Karen, my pet,
Oi! we're on fire!

Farewell architecture:
it's down to a cinder
for all those cowsheds decorated with cupids
and those rec halls in rococo!

O youth, phoenix, ninny,
your dissertation is hot stuff,
flirting its little red skirt now,
flaunting its little red tongue.

Farewell life in the sticks!
Life is a series of burned-out sites.

Nobody escapes the bonfire:
if you live—you burn.

But tomorrow, out of these ashes,
more poisonous than a bee
your compass point will dart
to sting you in the finger.

Everything's gone up in smoke,
and there's no end of people sighing.
It's the end?
                    It's only the beginning.
Let's go to the movies!

TRANSLATED BY STANLEY KUNITZ

GEORGIAN MARKETPLACES

Down with all Raphaels
and up with Flemish Rubens,
his fountains of fishtails,
his color and crudeness!

Here weekdays are feastdays
with oxcarts and gourds,
and women like tambourines
in bracelets and beads,

indigo of turkeys' wattles,
yellow *hurmas,* wine in bottles.
You're out of money?
Have a drink on me!

Bless all the old girls
who trade here in lettuce—
only baobab trees
boast a similar girth!

Marketplaces, blazes
of fire and youthfulness!
Your flaming bronzes
of hands are alight

with the gleam of butter
and the gold of wine.
Three cheers for the painter
who brings you alive!

TRANSLATED BY MAX HAYWARD

59

BALLAD OF THE FULL STOP

"A ballad? A ballad of the full stop? The knockout drop?"
You dope!
What about the bullet that punctuated Pushkin!

O the winds whistled as through the stops of clarinets
Through the perforated heads of our best poets,

Zinged on their course past oppression and piggishness
On a whistling trajectory hurtling down to posterity!
There was no full stop. It was all a beginning.

We go down into earth as through the gates of a railroad station,
And the O of the tunnel is as black as a muzzle . . .
What's the place we are heading for?
Immortality? Oblivion?

No death. No final dot. There's the path of the bullet—
A further propulsion of the same projectile.

Our sentence in nature has no period.
We shall be deathless.
                    And that's my point!

TRANSLATED BY STANLEY KUNITZ

5

THE TRIANGULAR PEAR

NEW YORK AIRPORT AT NIGHT

Façade

Guardian of heavenly gates, self-portrait, neon retort,
Airport!

Your Duralumined plate glass darkly shines
Like an X ray of the soul.

How terrifying
    when the sky in you
    is shot right through with the smoldering tracer lines
    of far-off capitals!

Round the clock
    your sluice gates
    admit the starred fates
    of porters and prostitutes.

    Like angels in the bar your alcoholics dim;
    Thou speakest with tongues to them.

Thou raisest them up
    who are downcast,
Thou who announcest to them at last:
      "Arrival!"

Landing Area

Cavaliers, destinies, suitcases, miracles are awaited . . .
Five Caravelles
    are slated
      dazzlingly to land from the sky.

Five fly-by-night girls wearily lower their landing gear;
Where is the sixth?

She must have gone too far—
      the bitch, the little stork, the star.

Cities dance under her
                like electric grills.

Where does she hover now,
                  circling around, moaning as though ill,
                  her cigarette glowing in the fog?

It's the weather she doesn't understand;
The ground won't let her land.

The Interior

The forecast is bad. When a storm looms,
You retreat, as with partisans, into your waiting rooms.

Our rulers snooze
                in carefree embrace
While the traffic controller, calm as a pharmacist, reroutes them
                          through the air.

One great eye peers into other worlds,
While with window cleaners
                like midges your other eyes water.

Crystal giant, parachuted from the stars,
It is sweet but sad
                to be the scion of a future that sports
Neither idiots
            nor wedding-cake railway stations—
Only poets and airports!

Groaning within its glass aquarium
The sky
          fits the earth like a drum.

Structures

Airport—accredited embassy
Of ozone and sun!

A hundred generations
                have not dared what you have won—
The discarding of supports.

In place of great stone idols
A glass of cool blue
              without the glass,
Beside the baroque fortresses of savings banks
As anti-material
         as gas.

Brooklyn Bridge, rearing its idiot stone, cannot consort
With this monument of the era,
The airport.

TRANSLATED BY WILLIAM JAY SMITH

THE TRIANGULAR PEAR

Prelude I

Be discovered, America!
Eureka!

I measure, explore,
                discover, all out of breath,

In America, *America*,
In myself, *myself*.

I peel the skin from the planet,
                      sweep away mold and dust;
Cut through the crust
           and go down
                  into the depths of things
As into the subway.

Down there grow triangular pears;
                  I seek the naked souls they contain.

I take the trapezoidal fruit, not to eat
Of it; but to let its glassy core
Glow with an altar's red heat.

Pry into it incessantly,
              do not relent;
Do not be misled
If they say your watermelon's green when in fact it's red.

I worry it like a retriever,
                hack at it like a cleaver!

And if the poet's a hooligan,
Then so was Columbus—carry on!

Follow your mad bent—
             head straight for shore . . .

You're looking for India—

                look a bit more—

You'll find

        America!

Prelude II

I adore
The blaze of your buildings, shooting up to the stars, to heaven's outskirts!

I am a greyhound
                    unleashed, a greyhound
Ready to hunt you down and learn your breed!

Below, past the storefronts
                  you race, a barefoot, beatnik girl!

And under the firehoses of thundering highways
                          my ears like millwheels whirl

Round over godless
                baseball-crazy
                    gasoline-hazy
                        America!

Coca-Cola.   Clangarola . . . Where
The hell am I?

Like hell—through penthouses, down alleyways and gutters—you led me on,
My eyes shooting back at women
                    like the bolts of guns!
From shopwindows your whoring goods hurled themselves at my neck.
But searching for your soul,
              I thrust them back,
And dived under Broadway, as with an aqualung.
A blue flame in a basement,
                one of your Negro women swayed!
I'd almost caught up with you
              but, quivering, you got away.

Read this and forgive:

> if I grasped nothing in the heat of the chase. . . .

A gnome on a roof I perch; below, New York, unfurled.
And your sun, on my little finger,

> sits like a ladybird.

TRANSLATED BY WILLIAM JAY SMITH

A BEATNIK'S MONOLOGUE
The Revolt of the Machines

Flee into yourself, to the Church, to the john, to Egypt, to Haiti—
flee!

Howling, caterwauling, hordes of fuming machines repeat
their cry: "Meat! Human meat!"

Machines as barbarous as Batu Khan
have enslaved us men.

In court the machine's insolent underlings,
swigging glasses filled with gasoline,
ponder: Who were those English fellows who led
a revolt against the machine?
Let us flee! . . .

And at night, mustering the courage,
a cybernetic robot
says to its creator:

"Give me your wife!
I have a weakness," it says, "for brunettes; I love them
at 30 rpm. It's best
to give up without protest."

O predatory creatures of our age,
the soul's been vetoed.
We retreat to the mountains, we hide in our beards.

We dive naked into water,
but the rivers are drying
up; in the seas the fish are dying.
Women will give birth to Rolls-Royces throughout the nation—
radiation.

My soul, helpless, hunted animal—
a puppy with a piece of rope

dangling from his neck—through the city's back alleys
you whine and mope.

And time whistles beautifully by
over fiery Tennessee—
enigmatic as a griffin
with a Duraluminum chassis.

TRANSLATED BY WILLIAM JAY SMITH

NEGROES SING

We,
>   Homeric tomtoms with doleful eyes, we wreathe
>>>   like smoke . . .

You,
>   white as refrigerators, absorbent cotton, deadlier white
>>>   than the dead . . .

of what can we sing to you, gentlemen?
of your hands waxen and white as chalk,
of how they left their print on sad shoulders, those hands,
of how they branded our wives with shame
>>   —O!

Whoa!
Beaten like nags, we beg for tips, in the ring and marketplace
our eyes dim,
but
in bed at night our backs, star-filled windows, gleam.

In us—
boxers, gladiators—as in black radiators,
reflected like carp in a pond, constellations swim,
solemnly, piteously—
the Bear and Mars
in us . . .

We Negroes, we poets,
in whom the planets splash,
lie like sacks full of legends and stars . . .
Trample upon us
and you kick the firmament.
The whole universe howls
beneath your boot!

TRANSLATED BY WILLIAM JAY SMITH

NEW YORK BIRD

On my windowsill,
monogrammed with moonlight,
                    perches
an aluminum bird;
in place of a body,
                    a fuselage.

And on its corkscrew neck
like the tongue of flame
on a giant cigarette lighter
blazes
          a woman's
                    face!

(Wound in his capitalistic sheet,
my traveling companion is asleep.)

Who are you? A cybernetic hallucination, who's
half robot, half creature of air?
A cross between a queen of the blues
and a flying saucer?

Perhaps you're the soul of America,
weary of playing, underneath?
Who are you, young Chimera,
that cigarette clenched between your teeth?

Unblinking, they stare
and steadily gleam—
the eyes like those of that girl somewhere
out in Chicago, face wreathed in cold cream,

circles under her eyes
as if by gas flames blurred—
What do you prophesy?
Don't lie to me, bird!

Will you communicate, will you report
what you know? Something strange from without

rises up in me
as in a branching retort—

the atomic age groans in this hotel room . . .

(I shout. And my companion, crying:
"You son of a bitch!" sits bolt upright in bed,
as if he'd been scalded.)

TRANSLATED BY WILLIAM JAY SMITH

ITALIAN GARAGE   *to Bella Akhmadulina*

The floor's a mosaic—
A trout's back stippled with light.

The garage in the palazzo sleeps.
                                    It is night.

In rows the motorcycles rest
Like Saracens or slumbering locusts.

No Paolos here, no Juliets—
Only Chevrolets that pant and sweat.

Figures in the Giotto frescoes are
Like mechanics mirrored in each car.

Ghosts of feuds and battles range at large;
What do you summon in your dreams, garage?

Is it halberds
                        or tyrants that haunt
You? Or women
                        picked up in restaurants?

One motorcycle seems to brood—
The reddest of the little brood.

Why is it still awake? Is it because
Tomorrow is Christmas and tomorrow it will crash?

Oranges, applause . . .
                        Those who smash
Themselves to pieces never die.

Give her the gun, doomed one, blood-red!
And for the girl who rides you it's too bad.

We were not born to survive, alas,
But to step on the gas.

TRANSLATED BY WILLIAM JAY SMITH

74

6

I'M A FAMILY OF SEVEN

I'm a family of seven,
I'm a spectrum resided in
by seven "I's" unbearable
as seven bears of whom
the bluest plays a pipe.
In springtime I imagine
I myself must be the eighth.

TRANSLATED BY MAX HAYWARD

THE NOSE

The nose grows during the whole of one's life.
(from scientific sources)

Yesterday my doctor told me:
"Clever you may be, however
Your snout is frozen."
So don't go out in the cold,
Nose!

On me, on you, on Capuchin monks,
According to well-known medical laws,
Relentless as clocks, without pause
Nose-trunks triumphantly grow.

During the night they grow
On every citizen, high or low,
On janitors, ministers, rich and poor,
Hooting endlessly like owls,
Chilly and out of kilter,
Brutally bashed by a boxer
Or foully crushed by a door,
And those of our feminine neighbors
Are foxily screwed like drills
Into many a keyhole.

Gogol, that mystical uneasy soul,
Intuitively sensed their role.

My good friend Buggins got drunk: in his dream
It seemed that, like a church spire
Breaking through washbowls and chandeliers,
Piercing and waking startled ceilings,
Impaling each floor like
Receipts on a spike,
Higher and higher

          rose

             his nose.

"What could that mean?" he wondered next morning.
"A warning," I said, "of Doomsday: it looks
As if they were going to check your books."
On the 30th poor Buggins was haled off to jail.

Why, O Prime Mover of Noses, why
Do our noses grow longer, our lives shorter,
Why during the night should these fleshly lumps,
Like vampires or suction pumps,
Drain us dry?

They report that Eskimos
Kiss with their nose.

Among us this has not caught on.

TRANSLATED BY W. H. AUDEN

You live with your aunt. She's addicted to ballads,
Snuffing and sneezing, thick in men's underpants.
How we hate the old bag!

Thank God the barn is our friend, that big
Amiable bear, hugging us warm,
With its breath of the bee house.

                And in Suzdal it's Easter! . . .
Old walled town holy with hubbub and ravens.

You whisper on my cheek about your childhood,
That country childhood blest by sun and horses,
And honeycombs gleaming like icons.
The gleam of honey is on your braids.

I live in Russia—among snows and saints!

TRANSLATED BY STANLEY KUNITZ

ODE TO GOSSIPS

I praise the keyhole,
Long live slanderers, may all
Reputations fall
Into a creaking bed.
O great tales, O gossips,
I love their regal lips,
Their ears like toilet bowls,
Pure white and infallible.

Fables gurgle and echo
Down the sewerage of years,
A writer's tomcat has swallowed
His neighbor's doves. I hear
Citizen X goes
Among the cabbages,
With ballerina Y . . .

I was living in Siberia, messages
From people I did not know
Came in like machine-gun bullets, flashes
Of gossip mowed me down, and as sopranos
Get carnations, I got letters and long-distance
Calls. Vanilla voices told of your hot romance.
His belly was fat, his hair flaming as his love,
You melted in his palms, an icicle on a hot stove.

I came home. On the streets of Moscow
It was almost spring—
Black streaks of melting snow.

It was all a lie—everything.
You wrapped your fur around you,
Smelled of snow and spring.

Darling Natasha, if anything
The slander confirmed your innocence.
By chance their lies came to prove
Your longing and your love.

Long live slanderers! Darlings, shout your heads off.
Lick your lips that have St. Vitus' dance.
But why this deathly silence?

They are no longer blaming or condemning.
The phone has stopped ringing.

TRANSLATED BY STANLEY MOSS

LILAC TREE

A lilac tree's like Paris,
aglow with wasps of windows
you stir a silver cluster
of wet and clammy houses.

Buzzing round with beetling brows,
grim with happiness and grief
I gather
       Paris
           like the bees
into the bags under my eyes.

TRANSLATED BY MAX HAYWARD

LAZINESS

Blessed is laziness my sweet trap,
I'm too lazy to get up, or fall back to sleep.

Too lazy to get the phone. You reach out,
your waist touches my shoulder. You're all in,

your leg is over me. I listen
to your breath born like a bell in your throat.

"What tickets?" To hell with them. This slow-
ness of days, within us, turns to shadow.

Progress is laziness:
the key to Diogenes is laziness!

You are too good to be true. What I know
is laziness. The world is impossible. Let it go.

Too lazy to get the cable: "push it under."
Too lazy to eat, or end the sentence: today is Sund . . .

June has flopped down here,
drunk in the middle of the road,
like a goat-legged satyr
barefoot and in shorts.

TRANSLATED BY STANLEY MOSS

PARIS WITHOUT RHYME

They're scrubbing Paris, making her spick and
span; they're blasting the city with sand,
scouring matrons in rococo,
treating them with the douche Charcot!

"High time too," I made bold to declare,
"to strip things of their outer layer,
to rid the world of all its cauls,
its fripperies and baroque walls!"

This wish of mine was made in fun,
but our worthy patron, Madame Lanchon,
said: "O la la, mon cher ami! . . ."
                                    and suddenly—

the town was transformed,
                walls vanished, or rather, became transparent.
Rooms hung over the streets like clusters of colored
                                                balloons,
each differently lit.
Inside, like pips of grapes,
                beds and people glowed.
Things threw off their protective covering:
on a table
some tea, preserving the form of its teapot, stood round and brown;
similarly, keeping the shape of its pipe,
                a tubular jet of water streaked across a ceiling.

They were celebrating mass in Notre Dame,
red cardinals and candelabra
gleamed through the glass of their aquarium
—the architecture had evaporated—
and only the great rose window
            hung over the square
            like a "One Way" sign.

On top of the Louvre the skeletons of the statues
quivered on their pedestals like sixteen mattress springs.

85

Springs were everywhere,
everything ticked.
O Paris,
       world of cobwebs, aerials, and bared wires,
how you quiver,
how you tick like a racing motor!
O heart under a purple membrane,
Paris
(in a breast pocket, vertical and fishlike
a Gillette razor floats past),
Paris, how easy it is to wound you, Paris,
under your covering of irony
you are so open as to be
almost defenseless,
Paris.

In Paris you're always alone,
but never by yourself,
and there's chagrin in your laughter,
                bitter as the stone in a cherry.
Paris is burning water,
Paris, how inside-out you are,
how white and fresh as bathing belles
are the barkless trees of your Bois de Boulogne
where dogs, skinless and pink, trot around
                    and sniff each other
in embarrassment—they seem to coalesce like beads of mercury.
And some creature, naked as a snake,
declares: "I am a silver fox."

People wander about without their heads
—they've been screwed off—
and their thoughts chirp
like birds in wire cages.

A nun is bothered by visions of something hairy and male;
the president of an all-male club fears public exposure
(his secret liaison with his wife has been uncovered
and he's been disgraced!);
a pair of pretty legs shimmers like a mirage over a traffic cop;
like a nimbus, a Wienerschnitzel on a silver platter

hovers above a poet in a *mansarde*;
in the fevered brain of an OAS man
Sartre is grilling on a frying pan,
while Sartre himself, our beloved Sartre,
pensive as a gentle grasshopper,
chews his cocktail straw
—the wise genius who presides over these mysteries.
Out of his straw, like a glassblower,
he blows these lanterns, the whole hollow town
with its *hôtels de ville* and *boucheries*,
as if they were so many soap bubbles!

I badger him: "Good Sartre,
conservatory not glassed in against winter weather,
why do your momentary bubbles
fly away so unprotected?

How terribly everything's exposed,
just a hairbreadth from fearful bruises
—even the air hurts like a rasp—
Good Sartre, suppose everything's condemned?"

The grasshopper sits silent on his leaf
with untold anguish on his face.
The clock strikes three . . .
Olga and I are sitting in the Crazy Horse,
sound in the form of a saxophone writhes between the lips of a jazzman.
A woman smirks:
"So it's striptease you want?" she says
and begins to peel off her dress, or rather—her skin!
—as one strips off stockings or tights.
Oh, oh! The last thing I remember were the whites
of her eyes, impassive as porcelain insulators
on that terrible flushed and screaming face . . .

". . . *mon ami*, your ice cream's melting . . ."
Paris . . . friends. The walls are back in place.
And outside, through all eternity
motorcyclists race in white helmets
—like hellhounds with pisspots on their heads.

TRANSLATED BY MAX HAYWARD

7
OZA

OZA

(A notebook found on the bedside table of a hotel in Dubna)

I

My fairhaired darling, what have I done?
This poem of mine will cause you pain?
I had hoped to make you live forever;
Instead, I have brought you only ruin.

That foolish cosmic egoist,
That drill sergeant, Goethe, deigned to command:
"Stop, moment, you are beautiful!"
No, Time—go on!—do not desist!

Why hobble life, as a horsethief will
A horse: our lives are mutually
Interactive, but immortality
Is halted motion: a film-still.

Immortality puts you behind bars;
Anna, Oza, and Beatrice—all are
Caged like animals while the public guffaws
And freely discusses their birthmarks.

Not seeing you now—how sad it
Is—seeing you only in a mob where
Every loudmouthed wretch can get his share
Of you—oh, the agony of it!

You will forgive me your pain and fret,
But you cannot forgive the lesions that bleed
In the soul, when anyone who can read
Drools over your life in the lines I write.

Let us say farewell through the bars of these lines:
I choke, the blood rushes to my head
When, like a butterfly caught in my hand,
Your voice comes fluttering on the telephone.

. . . . .

A woman stands by a cyclotron,
Graceful, fine-boned.

She listens, magnetized.
Light flows through her body
To the tip of her little finger
As red as a wild strawberry.

She still has her bracelet on,
She is changing, changing;
Now she's with us . . . now she's gone . . .
She seems to listen on and on.

Now she melts into thin air
And I fear for her fate!
It will soon be too late, too late
There by those Adam's apples,

those knobs of cyclotron 3-10-40.

I know that people consist of atoms and particles, just as rainbows consist
of shining specks of dust, or as sentences consist of letters. You only have to
change the order and your meaning changes.

I told her: don't go into the danger zone!
But she,
her nostrils quivering . . .
Is this a sacrificial offering
Or is she merely teasing,
Looking prettier than ever?

She still has her bracelet on,
She is changing, changing;
Now she's with us . . . now she's gone . . .
She seems to listen on and on.

"Zoya!" I shout. "Zoya!"
But she doesn't hear. She doesn't understand
Anything.

Perhaps her name is Oza?

II

I did not recognize my surroundings.

Things were just the same, but their particles, flashing, changed their shape, like the neon sign on top of the Central Telegraph Office. The connections between things were the same, but their direction was different.

Trees lay flat on the ground like leafy lakes, but their shadows stood upright like paper cutouts. They tinkled slightly in the wind, like silver bon-bon wrappings.

Now the shaft of a well shot upwards, like a black beam from a searchlight. A sunken bucket and bits of slime lay in it.

It was raining from three clouds, plastic combs with teeth of rain (two with teeth pointing downward, the other with teeth pointing upward).

A fine bit of castling! A Genoese tower has changed place with the belfry of Ivan the Great. The clinking icicles haven't even had time to melt.

The pages of history have been shuffled like a pack of cards. The Mongol invasion came after industrialization.

There was a line of people in front of the cyclotron, waiting to be serviced, to be taken apart and put together again. They came out transformed. One had an ear screwed to his forehead, with a hole in the middle, like a doctor's mirror. "Lucky devil," people consoled him, "very convenient for keyholes: you can look and hear at the same time!"

One lady asked for the manager. "They forgot to put my heart back. My heart!" With two fingers he pulled out her chest, like the right drawer of a desk, put something in it, and slammed it shut again. The Scientist sang and danced with glee.

"E-9-D4," murmured the Scientist. "Oh, great mystery of life! The whole does not change if its components are rearranged, as long as the system as such is preserved. Who cares about poetry? We shall have robots. The psyche is a combination of amino acids. . . .

"I've got an idea. Suppose we cut the earth in half along the equator, and put one hemisphere inside the other, like halves of an eggshell. . . . Of course, we would have to saw off the Eiffel Tower so it wouldn't puncture the surface in the region of the great Australian desert. True, half of mankind would perish, but the other half will get a kick out of the experiment."

The Board of the Quasi-Art Section was able to preserve order only on the platform. Its members shone like eggs in one of those illuminated display boxes in stores. They were all round and hence identical whichever way you looked at them. Except that one of them had his leg sticking up above the table where his torso should have been—like a periscope.

But nobody noticed this.

The speaker stuck his chest out. But his head, like a celluloid doll's, was back to front. "Forward to the Art of the Future!" Everybody agreed with him. But which way was forward?

An arrow (pointing perhaps to the toilet, or else to the Art of the Future) was sloping upwards like a minute hand at ten to three. People continued to walk along purposefully, Indian file, in the direction indicated, as though they were climbing an invisible stairway.

Nobody noticed anything.

NOBODY

Over all this, like an apocalyptic sign, there blazed a poster:
Beware of Careless Connections! But the tacks were sticking wrong side out.

NOTICED

ANYTHING

Perhaps her name is Oza?

III

At dawn in my sleep,
My dear, I see you now,
Flying, with gun barrels
Trained on you from below,

Over the marshes near Moscow,
Chillingly beautiful,
Thirty meters of ozone
Your only camouflage!

Your moments are numbered
By the bullets in those guns;
All your armor and defense,
Thirty meters of ozone.

Flying is without joy
In that marshy dawn,
But with her heart set on it,
There's no holding her down.

Lord, let me have wings
Not for glorious fame,

But just to protect her
From their deadly aim!

Let her go roaring on
On her social round,
One fling, one second more,
But let her not look round.

May she even end happily,
Married, mother of a child.
Do I see her really?
Does she still come in dreams?

Do I see her morning to night
There with her carefree set,
Up all night, or only at dawn
Just before the bullets hit?

IV

We're too sentimental for our own good;
Souls will be removed just as tonsils should.

Will that silvery flutist, your precious iamb,
Die as trout die at the foot of a dam?

Is love like the fireplace out of date?
Goodbye to all that?

Then why, when we pack the Luzhniki,
Do we crave verse like a cure for scurvy,
Our souls bursting shyly forth like buds? . . .
Robots,
          robots,
                    robots
Interrupt my words.

Files of automata
Troop to the slots,
Put in their coins,
Take what they get.

There's no time to think;
We're loaded like tin cans
In offices, gross and net;
No time to be human.

A country girl stirred
In a poet's bed
One morning and said
"We'd no time for a word!"

You'd wish, when you woke
Like country folk,
Fairy tales, rhyme?
No time, no time.

What kicks in my chest
Like a partisan girl?
Heart, you can rest
In this automated world.

My God! Mother,
                bear me back! . . .

Back to their sources flow the rivers.
Back—from the finishing post to the starting line, in reverse, race the motorcyclists.
Baobab trees, under our very eyes, shrink and turn back into saplings!
That bullet whips out of Mayakovsky's heart, through the hole burnt in his shirt, back into the barrel of Mauser 4-03986, which, curling up like a snail, drops into the drawer of the desk. . . .

. . . Your father's a historian. He says that mankind has reverse age, that it advances from old age to youth.

Take the Middle Ages. This was really old age. Look at the wrinkled walls of the Inquisition.

Then came the Renaissance, mankind's Indian summer. It was like a woman, beautiful and all-knowing, banqueting amidst ripe fruit and bodies.

". . . the electron is considered to be scattered backward in time from

t_2 to t_1. Then the conventional positron becomes an electron going backward in time."
—R. P. Feynman, *Theory of Fundamental Processes*, New York, 1961

We won't bother to catalogue the hopes, betrayals, and adventures of the
18th century, nor will we dwell on the brooding pregnancy of the 19th. But
the beginning of the 20th with its frantic rhythm of revolution and army
commanders aged eighteen! "We are the earth's first love." "Socialism, live,
human, and true, is now coming about." But this was not all . . . :

Does a high wind make me reel
Or does memory unwind like a spool?
I hear on a record player
A vile marching air.

Of Stalin do not sing;
That is no simple song,
But mixed like his gray mustaches,
Cloudy at times, then clear.

They looped about the pipe
Of the Great Engineer,
Nuts and bolts surveying,
Blind to human beings.

How many were impounded,
Needles in that gray stack,
Stroked when the anthem sounded,
Dipped in wine blood-red?

Majestic over the land,
The wings of a bird of prey,
They hovered,
                    tinged with red,
Great mustaches of state.

Of Stalin do not sing;
We are more than nuts and bolts;
And no more shall we choke
On his blue-bearded smoke.

97

"I am thinking of a future," the historian continues, "when all dreams
will come true. In good hands technology is good. Afraid of technology?
Very well, go back to the caves then!"
He is gray-haired and rosy-cheeked. Children and dogs smile at him.

AUTHOR'S NOTE AND ONE OR TWO OTHER THINGS

I love Dubna. I have friends there.
Birches grow, splitting the paved sidewalks;
And the gaze of the wonderful inhabitants
Is just as independent, as fluid as air.

The scientific giants are bearded like trees,
And perhaps if I do not come to a bad end,
I will owe it to Dubna, protector and friend,
As I live to protect its luminous trees.

It is for their sake I am here.
I found a diary at a hotel there.

I'm not the first to read this notebook,
Other guests have been through it before,
Scribbling their wisecracks in the margin
And gone to sleep, trying to make it out.

One scrawl: "The author's an abstractionist—take him away!"
Below, in red, someone has added: "The hell you say!"

"Perhaps the author is one of those
Who titillate their readers with hidden meanings?"

"Stop hunting for hidden meaning, wise guy,
A fat lot you can see in *anything* you read."

But enough of these gems for today, diary,
We already have more comment than we need!

V

Why not let us be off to the seashore?

VI

Once upon a midnight dreary, while, at low tide, weak and weary,
I held forth to my friends on Oza and the glories of creation.
Suddenly there came a raven, breaking up that conversation;
Flashing eyes of fearful black,
           Quoth the raven, "What the hell!"

"Bird!" I cried. "I'm pained at seeing you are not a human being
To help us carve the world in two . . . to join us in this blissful work."
           Quoth the raven, "What the hell!"

"Just think what you could be, great mentor, god of machines, experimenter,
You'd live in bronze, O great inventor, world-renowned . . . What
                         wondrous luck!"
           Quoth the raven, "What the hell!"

"Constructing great machines, you'd build democracy and make it work,
Ridding the world of useless kings and queens . . . and all such crud."
           Quoth the raven, "What the hell!"

"Or you might," quoth I, "one day have a cottage far away
Where a girl's sweet fingertips would place cherries on your lips,
A cottage so remote you'd never hear a word of praise or blame. . . ."

Quoth the raven, "Don't be a ninny, you are the slave if there ever
                         was any;
You are free but have no freedom however free you may appear;
You race ahead in a powerful car, but it has no wheel with which
                         to steer.

Oza, Rosa, or some other whore
                         —these transformations, what a bore.
           Sooner or later, they'll lie in the muck. . . .
Life is short, so what the hell?"

How explain to this vile croaker
That we are here not just to croak,
But to touch with living tongue
Wondrous lips and clear-cold brooks?

To live is so great a miracle,
How argue with those who never will?

One could, I suppose, but what the hell?

VII

You are seventeen. You are out of breath after all that exercise. And it doesn't matter what your name is. You've never even heard of a cyclotron.

Some idiot has stuck two mercury lamps on the seafront here. We are walking towards each other. You start from one of the lamps and I set out from the other. We each have a beam of light trained on our backs.

And before our hands touch, our shadows merge—they are alive, warm and fringed with a deathly pallor.

You still seem to be coming towards me.

The nape of one's neck always looks to the past. Time stretches out behind us, like a line of people waiting for a trolley-bus. I have the past behind me—it's as though I had a rucksack on my shoulders. But you have the future behind you—it makes a noise like a parachute.

When we are together I feel the future flowing from you into me, and the past flowing from me into you—as though we were an hourglass.

How you loathe relics of the future! You are impetuous, straightforward, and amazingly ignorant.

For you the past is something still to come about and subject to change. "Napoleon," I say, for instance, "won the battle of Austerlitz," and you reply: "We shall see."

The future, on the other hand, you find much more certain. Here, everything is foregone conclusion:

"We are going to the woods tomorrow," you say, and what a wood it was that rustled in our ears the next day! You still have a dry pine needle in your left shoe.

Your shoes have sharply pointed toes—people don't wear them like that any more. "*Still* don't wear them like that," you laugh back at me.

I try to shield you from the past with my body, so that you will never see Majdanek and the Inquisition.

Your teeth are pink with lipstick.

Sometimes you nestle up to me. I see you have something on your mind and I ask: "Well, what is it?" Leaving my arms and very pleased with yourself, you rattle off a phrase, as though it were in a foreign language: "That gave me great aesthetic pleasure! And to think I used to be afraid of you. . . . A penny for your thoughts! . . ."

Ah, my thoughts, my thoughts, my thoughts. . . .
Where is she now?

Supposing her name is Oza?

VIII

When I walk in the park or swim in the sea,
A pair of her shoes waits there on the floor.

The left one leaning on the right,
Not enough time to set them straight.

The world is pitch-black, cold and desolate,
But they are still warm, right off her feet.

The soles of her feet left the insides dark,
The gold of the trademark has rubbed off.

A pair of red doves pecking seed,
They make me dizzy, rob me of sleep.

I see the shoes when I go to the beach
Like those of a bather drowned in the sea.

Where are you, bather? The beaches are clean.
Where are you dancing? With whom do you swim?

In a world of metal, on a planet of black,
Those silly shoes look to me like

Doves perched in the path of a tank, frail
And dainty, as delicate as eggshell.

IX

. . . At this point come some lecture notes,
A mass of figures, and someone's profile;
The doodler, though, is scarcely a realist,
He's no Repin, our unknown artist.

Beyond this, some pages have been removed.
Some earlier reader, in a drunken fit,
Must have ripped out the juiciest bit. . . .
The diary resumes with a sentence beginning

                                                    YOU

                    X

You are celebrating your birthday today—the 16th—in the banquet room
of the Berlin. The ceiling there has a mirror.
The guests hang head downwards from the ceiling. A pink wedding cake with
candles stuck in it hangs down, like an udder, from the center of the
ceiling.
       Round about it, like electric bulbs screwed into the black sockets
of their suits and dresses, bald pates and hairdos glow. One can't see their
faces. One of them has a small bald patch, no bigger than a hole in the heel
of a stocking—you could block it out with black ink.
       Another bald head is as translucent as a ripe apple and through the
skin you can see—like pips—three thoughts: two of them black, and the
third light in color: it has not yet matured.
       The partings of well-groomed hair shine like the slits in piggy
banks.
       The neck of a brunette with a transparent nylon band pinned to it
glides over the ceiling like a fly.
       One can't see their faces. But they have cards in front of them giving
their names, as though they have been labeled like exhibits in a museum.
       Only one plate is white and empty.
       "Tell me," someone asks. "Why is the place next to our hostess
vacant?"
       —"Perhaps they're waiting for a general? Or perhaps somebody's
died?"
       Nobody realizes that I am sitting there. I am invisible. All those elegant
fellows coming up to wish you many happy returns bump into me and
scratch me with their forks.
       You are sitting there next to me, but you are splendidly remote, like
a gift wrapped in cellophane.
       People beg a fashionable poet: "Do let's have something—you know
what: something close to life, something out of this world . . . as long as
it's modern. . . ."
       The poet gets up (or rather, drops down, in the way a rope ladder is

lowered from a helicopter). His voice is strange and, so to speak, antiworldly, as though he were only intoning somebody else's words.

A PRAYER

Blessed Virgin of Vladimir, our one and only,
For the first time and the last I plead;
Thou, whose eyes are high and lonely,
I entreat Thee now to intercede.

I'm at the end of my tether—that is all,
I do not intend any blasphemy;
My life, my success, this clearest voice in all
Russia—what good are they now to me?

All is vanity before her fair hair;
All hope is lost. . . .
                    Throw Thyself at her feet,
Holy Mother of Vladimir, I entreat
Thee:
            Move her, and save me from despair.

As he reads, he throws back his head and his nose shines on the white plate of his face like a Bulgarian red pepper.

People shout: "Bravo! He's the best of the lot! Here's to him."

He is followed by another poet who is dead drunk. He hangs down from the ceiling like a towel drying on a clothes line. It is only possible to make out a few muttered words:

Beyond Lake Onega
                    a steamer slips away.
Let me dive deep into your lake now.
Pre-Ozian was all my life until now,
Into Trans-Ozia may I not like that steamer stray.

Everybody is silent.

The next to speak is X, the Toastmaster.

He swings head downwards as though he were a pendulum. "I give you the health of our guest of honor." His voice booms from the ceiling like a loudspeaker. "Here's many happy returns to her and, as her godfather, I . . . what's her name now?" (Nobody knows.)

103

It is all vaguely familiar. Under this world suspended on the ceiling there is a second world, an upside-down one, which also has its poet and its toastmaster. The napes of their necks almost touch—they are counterpoised like the two halves of an hourglass. But what is all this and where are we? In what preposterous dimension? What is this reality reflected in the ceiling? What is this upside-down country?

Lost in these thoughts, I absentmindedly started eating a red-caviar sandwich. Why is that provincial celebrity, who hangs opposite me like a smoked ham, looking at my stomach with such horror? God, how stupid! I'd clean forgotten that I am invisible, but that sandwiches aren't—this was something that H. G. Wells warned us about. The celebrity moves a little closer towards me.

He whispers in his neighbor's ear and immediately heads are threaded together by rumor as beads on a string.

Red snakes of tongues dart into neighboring ears. Everybody looks at my caviar sandwich.

"And all *we* get is sardines!" the celebrity hisses.

I must hide! If they catch me, who will save you, who will smash the mirror?

I jump up from the table and lie flat on the floor, which has a red carpet. Next to me, behind a chair, I see a pair of shoes. They must have been slipped off because they hurt. The left one has fallen against the right one (how familiar it all is!). People ask you to sing something. . . .

Now they've begun to dance. The soles of their shoes! The first couple passes over me with a crunch. Why do they all have studs on their soles? Somebody tramples on the little shoes next to me. A pair of heels goes rat-a-tat-tat over the skin of my face as though it were being stitched by a sewing machine. As long as they don't get my eyes!

I remember it all in a flash—
The robots, the robots, the robots.

The way you appear in my dreams, dear!
"Well, what's her name?" asks the flustered Toastmaster. . . .

"Zoya," I yell, "Zoya!"

But perhaps her name is Oza?

XI

Come, Zoya, let us now talk straight—
Our paths are about to separate;
If in different ways they tend,
It's the beginning of the end.

You remember Dubna, Zoya, swathed in white,
You were playing the piano, remember?
You turned round from the keyboard, remember?
And your face was utterly empty and white;
Something in it was not there any more,
Something that no one can restore.

I've been through much: rain and rainbows equally,
The horizon has frowned upon my name;
Friends took pleasure in betraying me.
I was even completely sick of myself;
But through it all you remained the same.

Do you remember my farewell reading?
You came to my rescue when they jeered;
If I am alive, whatever they claim,
It is you who are to thank or blame.

When trouble licked at me like flame,
I dived into Riga, as one would into water,
And through a straw as fair as your hair,
You gave me your breath and your breath was air.

Kilometers do not separate,
Like telephone wires they unite;
It is a more unpardonable fate
If it's only millimeters that divide.

If it's true that trouble draws us closer,
Then why should I want ever to be free
Of it; and suppose that it is you, not I,
Who is really being stalked by trouble?

Those who save us are not safe themselves;
Whatever ordeals I may have to go through,

What really concerns me is not myself
But rather how I can protect you.

Is it you who are changing—or is it I?
From all our past, those other years,
The shapes of the people we once were
Wave after us now dejectedly.

XII

The Scientist, damn his eyes,
Has invented a god-damned machine;
I can't keep up with what goes on—
Damn all you cyclotrons.

Damn you, you blasted pile
Of programmed animals;
Let me be damned for passing, too,
As the poet of your particles.

The world is not junk up for auction.
I am Andrei, not just anyone.
All progress is retrogression
If the process breaks man down.

We can't be bought by a silly toy,
By some mechanical nightingale,
The main thing in life is human kindness:
Is it sorrow you feel, or joy?

Russia, my country, home of beauty,
Land of Rublev, Blok, and Lenin,
Where the snow falls enchantingly
As pure and white as the purest linen.
She has no higher calling
          than to
                bring the world
                        to safety!

I curse all this pseudo-progress,
My throat is sore from technical terms;

Having given them voice and soul,
I'll be damned for the fact a woman will,

Bolting down her food capsules,
One day in the future, ask someone:
"In Volume 3 of Voznesensky,
What is that creature, the cyclotron?"

I answer: "Its bones have rusted away;
It's no more scary than a troika racing by:
Technologies and states live for a day,
Then go their way, and pass us by."

Only one thing on earth is constant
Like the light of a star that has gone;
It is the continuing radiance
They used to call "the human soul."

We shall melt away and again be there;
It matters little when or where.

What matters is to live, as bright as woods
When frost has cleared the morning sky
And all the bushes are tinkling with berries.
In their clear sound I shall not die.

And the woman then will think: "How strange!
I remember Dubna, and the campfires on the snow.
My fingers were red from the ski poles.
The piano keys were icy-cold.

I wonder what ever became of Zoya?"

                    "You mean that physicist . . . why?"

Goodbye, goodbye.

Remotely, as through glass,
You stare, fresh and bright.
The world is sunny and cold. . . .

Farewell, Zoya.
            Greetings, Oza!

    XIII

ON THE VERANDA,
CLEANING THE SNOW FROM MY SKIS,
                    I RAISED MY HEAD.
AN AIRPLANE WAS FLYING OVERHEAD.
BEHIND IT, ALWAYS AT THE SAME DISTANCE,
THE SOUND TRAILED,
RECTANGULAR, LIKE A BARGE BEHIND
                    A TUG.

    XIV

Hail, Oza, at night when at home,
Or away somewhere, wherever it may be,
And dogs are howling, licking up their tears,
It is the sound of your breathing I hear.
        Hail, Oza!

Cynic and clown, how could I have known,
Like one who timidly steps into a lake,
That love in reality is fear.
        Hail, Oza!

You—people, locomotives, germs,
Be as careful with her as you can.
I would not have her come to harm.
        Hail, Oza!

If Life is not just a vegetable, then
Why is it sliced and shredded by men?
        Hail, Oza!

How tragic that we met so late,
How far more tragic to be separate.

Opposites have been drawn together.
Let me absorb your bitterness and pain;

I am the sad pole of the magnet;
You are the bright one. May you so remain.

May you never know how sad I am.
I shall not distress you with myself.
I shall not trouble you with my death,
I shall not burden you with my life.

Hail, Oza, may you stay bright
Like the light behind a lantern slide.
I cannot blame you now for having left,
But thank you for having come into my life.

Dubna—Odessa
March 1964

VERSE TRANSLATED BY WILLIAM JAY SMITH
PROSE TRANSLATED BY MAX HAYWARD

NOTES

Andrei Voznesensky's poetry has been published in the following collections: *Mozaika* (Vladimir, 1960), *Parabola* (Moscow, 1960), *Scrivo come amo (Pishetsya kak lyubitsya)* (Milan: Feltrinelli, 1962), *Treugol'naya grusha* (Moscow, 1962), and *Antimiry* (Moscow, 1964). Hereafter these books will be referred to by the abbreviations in parentheses: *Mozaika (M), Parabola (P), Scrivo come amo (SCA), Treugol'naya grusha (TG),* and *Antimiry (AM).*

The editors will have occasion to refer frequently to the monthly magazines *Znamya (Z)* and *Molodaya gvardiya (MG).*

1   I AM GOYA

I AM GOYA

Published in identical form in *M, SCA,* and *AM.*

This is one of the poet's favorites, and he always recites it at his public readings. It provides a good example of his use of assonance: *Ya Góya . . . nagóye . . . ya góre . . . ya gólos . . . góda . . . ya gólod . . . ya górlo . . . góloi.*

MY ACHILLES HEART

Published in the monthly magazine *Yunost* (No. 6, 1965).

It seems clear that the "crack shots" in this poem must refer to some of the people who took part in the campaign against Voznesensky in 1963 (see Introduction).

WALL OF DEATH

Published with insignificant variants in *Z* (No. 4, 1962), *SCA, TG,* and *AM.* Our text is taken from *AM.*

The spelling of "Singichants" in the *AM* variant identifies the name as Armenian; it probably refers to a trainer in the Moscow Circus, which has a "Wall of Death." The dedication has been omitted in *Z* and *SCA.* In his readings, Voznesensky identifies N. Androsova as a "Master of Sport of the Soviet Union" (an honorary title given to prize sportsmen and sportswomen).

HUNTING A HARE

Published in *AM.*

The poem is dedicated to the well-known Russian short-story writer Yuri Kazakov, who is also the Yuri of the poem.

The character named Bukashkin (here rendered in English as Buggins) appears in two other poems by Voznesensky, "Antiworlds" and "The Nose." Bukashkin is the poet's image of the archetypal downtrodden clerk—a kind of Soviet Walter Mitty whose humdrum and somewhat haunted existence is relieved only by fantasies and excursions of the kind described in these three poems. The name, like that of Gogol's Akaki Akakievich (whom he resembles), is comically in tune with his personality. It is derived from *bukashka,* meaning a small insect, and corresponds to the English surname Buggins.

The "jalopy" *(gazik)* is the classic car made in the Gorky Auto Works (GAZ). The word has now come to stand for any old car.

"Tallyho!" is the translator's rendering of *trali-vali,* a similar expression used by sailors. It is also the title of a story by Kazakov.

THE SKULL BALLAD

Published in *Z* (No. 4, 1962), *TG,* and *AM.* Our text is from *AM.*

In *Z* the poem is titled "A Digression into March, 1719. The Skull Ballad." In *TG* this has been changed to "A Digression into the Seventeenth Century. The Skull Ballad." In *AM* the title is simply "The Skull Ballad."

Stanley Kunitz's translation is rather free; it gives approximate equivalents for expressions and concepts which would have little meaning to a person who has not been brought up in the Soviet Union. For example, "dirty foreigner" stands for "Anglo-Swedish-German-Greek spy." In 1937–38, many Russians were falsely accused of being multiple agents of this kind.

The woman being executed by Peter the Great in the "Place of Skulls" *(Lobnoye mesto)* on Red Square—hence the title of the poem—is Anna Mons, who was for a time his favorite in the latter part of the seventeenth century. An invidious attempt to decipher the poem was made by the critic V. Nazarenko (*Zvezda*, No. 6, 1962), who suggested that Voznesensky deliberately invented the beheading of Anna Mons (she actually died a natural death), inserted anachronisms, such as "motorbike," and used typically Soviet terminology (such as *stroitel'stvo*, meaning "construction," as in "Socialist construction") in order to "express certain ideas of universal application." "We have here, in allegorical form," Nazarenko wrote, "gloomy reflections on the allegedly tragic fate of the individual supposedly crushed by social laws . . . on an eternal and universal scale. The message of *The Triangular Pear* [the collection in which "The Skull Ballad" appeared] is that the world is immutable and that everything will remain as it always was—that man is eternal and the tragedy of the individual is eternal."

In his preface to *TG*, Voznesensky wrote: "Poems have a life and character of their own. Occasionally, against the author's will, they balk at grammar. This is sometimes the result of the fantastic nature of the theme. For instance, a severed head begins to speak. No time for punctuation here!"

SOMEONE IS BEATING A WOMAN

Published with no significant variants in Z (No. 4, 1962), *TG*, and *AM*.

THE CASHIER

Published with no significant variants in *M* and *SCA*. Our text is from *SCA*.

In *M* the poem is dedicated to D. N. Zhuravlev.

The setting of this poem is a large Soviet (and, of course, state-owned) grocery store. In such stores, the woman cashier ordinarily sits inside a kind of glass booth at her cash desk.

When the cashier holds up a bill to the light, she is looking for the watermark of Lenin's head which appears on Soviet bank notes.

2   GIVE ME PEACE

AUTUMN IN SIGULDA

Published with some variants in Z (No. 4, 1962), *SCA*, *TG*, and *AM*. Our text is from *TG*.

The most important variant appears in the first published version, in Z. Here the final line (omitted in all later versions) is: "Hold her back" *(Ee uderzhite)*, which would give the impression that the previous line, the literal meaning of which is "Save!" *(Spasite!)*, is a call to save the woman, and not a personal cry for help. All the other versions require the latter interpretation.

Sigulda is a summer resort in Latvia.

"Let us sit here a bit" (line 22) has a double significance. It is both an expression of the poet's concern for his weary mother and an allusion to the Russian superstition that one should sit down for a moment before leaving a place where one has lived.

"Goodbye" (line 24) is in English in the Russian original. Like many other foreign expressions, "goodbye" is a commonplace in Russian colloquial speech, especially among teen-agers.

"In cold stone" (line 42) renders *bul'dik*, a slang word for a stone.

"Some old underworld song" (line 53) refers to the extremely popular type of song (for which there is no Western equivalent) that first arose out of the underworld of Odessa. Such songs were sung in Russian *cafés chantants* before and immediately after the Revolution. They were suppressed as decadent under Stalin but became popular again after his death.

DEAD STILL

Published in Z (No. 6, 1965).

The poem was written after the major attacks on Voznesensky in 1963 (see Introduction).

FIRST FROST

Published in identical form in *P, SCA,* and *AM.*

AM dates the poem 1959.

AUTUMN

Published with some insignificant variants in *M, P, SCA,* and *AM.* Our text is from *M.*

The poem is dedicated to the poet S. Shchipachev.

THE PARTY

Published in identical form in *M* and *SCA.*

YOU SIT, PREGNANT AND PALE . . .

Published in identical form in *M, SCA,* and *AM.*

AM dates the poem 1958.

"To nearby towns or vast Siberia" (line 12) renders the more specific place names Khabarovsk, in eastern Siberia, and Lyubertsy, near Moscow.

Ashkhabad (line 13) is the capital of the Turkmen SSR.

BICYCLES

Published with some differences in punctuation in *P, SCA,* and *AM.* Our text is from *SCA.*

Victor Bokov, to whom the poem is dedicated, is a Russian poet.

HOMELESS

Published in *Literaturnaya gazeta,* August 7, 1965.

"Priests" in line 11 renders *skhimniki,* Russian Orthodox monks who distinguish themselves by their asceticism. The reference in this context is apparently to icons.

GIVE ME PEACE

Published in *AM.*

"Shepherds" in the seventh stanza renders the more specific *chabany,* used of shepherds in the south of the country, mainly in the Crimea.

3 WHO ARE WE?

FOGGY STREET

Published with variants in *M, SCA,* and *AM.* Our text is from *M.*

AM dates the poem 1959.

THE LAST TRAIN TO MALAKHOVKA

Published in *M, SCA,* and *P* with some variants. Our text is from *M,* which is identical with *SCA.*

Malakhovka, a suburb of Moscow, has a bad reputation. The last train back from Moscow might well include among the passengers juvenile delinquents, criminals, and prostitutes.

"Gold-crowned smiles" *(fiksy)* in line 2 refers to the fashion for girls to have crowns put on healthy teeth—a symbol of status in some circles.

In the fifth stanza the poem recited is evidently "First Frost" (p. 23).

STRIPTEASE

Published in Z (No. 4, 1962), *SCA, TG,* and *AM.* Our text is from *AM.*

This poem, like many others in the "Triangular Pear" cycle, evokes an image or impression from Voznesensky's visit to the United States in 1961. "Striptease" may be compared with "Prelude I" (p. 66), in which the poet also is engaged in a search for the essence of America. The implication of the last four lines seems to be that the answer to his question "Are you America?" is not as simple as it is sometimes made out to be.

In the last line, the Russian text calls for a mixture of martini and absinthe (*absent* rhyming with *aktsent*), which is clearly unfeasible in English. It has therefore been rendered as "double martini."

TRIPTYCH

Published in SCA and AM with no substantial differences. Our text is from AM. We have taken the title from SCA. AM has no title.

Mikhailovskoye (line 2) was the Pushkin family estate to which the poet was exiled in 1824.

The "three pine trees" (line 3) are mentioned in Pushkin's famous poem "... Vnov' ya posetil ..." which is concerned with the poet's exile to Mikhailovskoye, where the three pine trees grow.

Matroshkas (line 10) are painted wooden female dolls in peasant dress. They are of graduated size and fit into one another.

ANTIWORLDS

Published in Z (No. 4, 1962), TG, and AM with a few variants. Our text is from Z.

The AM version has no title and is listed in the index under the poem's first line. For "Bukashkin," see note on "Hunting a Hare."

The "deserts" referred to in line 15 are, specifically, in the Russian, the Kara-Kum or Black Sands of Central Asia.

In the fifth line from the bottom, "total loss" renders *mura*, a slang word for something boring and meaningless.

GEORGIAN ROADS

Published in identical form in M and SCA.

The poem refers to the nineteenth-century Russian poets, the best known of whom is Lermontov (1814–41), who were sent on active army service in the Caucasus as a form of punishment for political and other misdemeanors.

MARCHÉ AUX PUCES

Published in Z (No. 11, 1963) and AM with insignificant variants. Our text is from Z.

The "grains of sand" in the last three lines of section 2 refer to an old method of destroying the enemy's guns by putting sand in the barrels. When fired, the barrels exploded.

The poem was written after Voznesensky's trip to Paris and a visit to Picasso in the winter of 1962.

WHO ARE WE?

Published with insignificant variants in M, SCA, and AM. Our text is from AM, but omits lines 13 and 14 in accordance with the text as ordinarily recited by the poet. The lines omitted are: I, ottaivaya ladoshki, / Poetessy begut v lotoshnitsy! ("And, warming their hands, / Poetesses run off to be street vendors!")

AM dates the poem 1959. In M and SCA the title is "Who Are You?" In AM the poem has no title and is indexed by its first line.

The contrast drawn between "physicist" and "lyricist" (line 2) is like that drawn between the "two cultures" in the West. The physicist-lyricist controversy has become a commonplace of Soviet literary discussion in the 1960's.

It should be noted, in connection with the third stanza ("an architect turned into a poet"), that Voznesensky was originally trained as an architect.

"Half-world streets of Moscow" (line 18) renders the more specific Stoleshnikov Street, which has acquired an unsavory reputation.

4 THE PARABOLA

PARABOLIC BALLAD

Published with some variants in M, P, SCA, and AM. Our version is taken from SCA.

The M and AM versions are the same, except for some differences in punctuation. SCA differs from M and AM in one important respect, in that the third line from the end in SCA reads: "He is leaving tonight for Siberia." M and AM have "In the Siberian spring galoshes sink" (V Sibirskoi vesne utopayut kaloshi ...). The P version leaves out the last six lines altogether, beginning "Laughing at law ..."

BALLAD OF 1941

Published in M and P. Our version is from M, but the last stanza has been omitted in accordance with a version read by the poet in public.

The M version is dedicated to the partisans of Kerch, a peninsula in the Crimea, where a group of partisans hid underground in old stone quarries during World War II.

The seventh stanza in M has been omitted in P.

LEAVES AND ROOTS

Published in the newspaper Literatura i zhizn (November 20, 1960), SCA, and AM with some variants. Our text is from SCA.

Although the poem was first published on the fiftieth anniversary of the death of Leo Tolstoy, it would also seem to have been written in memory of Boris Pasternak. The SCA version is explicitly dedicated to the memory of Tolstoy. AM, which bears no dedication, dates the poem 1960.

SCA is the only version with the line "There is not a soul in Russia." The other two versions have "in the neighborhood" (v okruge).

MASTER CRAFTSMEN

Published with some variants in M, P, SCA, and AM. Our text is from AM.

Only the first two parts of this long poem, which consists of two "dedications" and seven "chapters," have been translated.

Barma was one of the architects of St. Basil's Cathedral on Red Square, built in the reign of Ivan the Terrible. According to a legend, the Czar had the eyes of the architects gouged out so they could never again build anything as beautiful.

Moabit is a jail in Berlin.

Zoya in the "First Dedication" is Zoya Kosmodemyanskaya, a Russian heroine of World War II who was tortured and executed by the Germans.

THE TORCHES OF FLORENCE

Published with some variants in the magazine Yunost (No. 1, 1963) and in AM. Our text is from Yunost.

This poem is one of a number based on the poet's visits to Italy in the early 1960's. Here the poet ironically contrasts the poor architectural student he once was with what he has become—a successful public figure who gives press conferences when abroad. In the second stanza, he mocks his own early designs, conceived in the spirit of the wild eclecticism of Stalinist architecture. (See note on "Fire in the Architectural Institute.")

FIRE IN THE ARCHITECTURAL INSTITUTE

Published with some variants in SCA and TG. Our text is from TG.

SCA has raikluby (rec halls) instead of sberkassy (savings banks) in the sixth stanza. The translator has preferred to follow the SCA version in his rendering of this line. This stanza refers ironically to the architecture of the Stalin era, when public buildings were designed in a variety of incongruous styles.

It should be noted that there actually was a fire at the Moscow Architectural Institute when Voznesensky was a student there. The fire consumed his designs together with his career as an architect.

GEORGIAN MARKETPLACES

Published in identical form in *P* and *AM*. The title given in *P* is "Gruzinskie bazary" ("Georgian Bazaars"). The title given in *AM* is "Tbilisskie bazary" ("Tbilisi Bazaars").

Hurmas are fruit of the persimmon family that grow in the Caucasus.

BALLAD OF THE FULL STOP

Published in identical form in *M, SCA,* and *AM*.

The untimely death of poets is a well-known feature of Russian literary history. Among the poets "punctuated" by bullets were Pushkin and Lermontov (in duels) and Mayakovsky (by suicide).

5   THE TRIANGULAR PEAR

NEW YORK AIRPORT AT NIGHT

Published with some variants in *Z* (No. 4, 1962), *SCA, TG,* and *AM*. Our text is from *Z*.

In "Structures" the last lines ("Brooklyn Bridge, rearing its idiot stone . . .) echo and respond to the poem "Brooklyn Bridge" (1925) by Mayakovsky, who celebrated the bridge as a triumph of modern technology.

THE TRIANGULAR PEAR

Published with some variants in *Z* (No. 4, 1962) and *TG*. Only "Prelude II" appears in *SCA*. Our text is from *Z*.

The editors have supplied the general title "The Triangular Pear" from the collection in which these poems appeared.

A BEATNIK'S MONOLOGUE

Published with some variants in *Z* (No. 4, 1962), *SCA, TG,* and *AM*. Our text is from *Z*.

In *Z* the poem is titled: "A Beatnik's Monologue. The Revolt of the Machines." In *SCA*: "The Revolt of the Machines." In *AM*: "A Beatnik's Monologue." In *TG* it appears together with another poem on the same subject, under the general title "Digression in the Form of Beatnik's Monologues." In *Z* there is a misprint in line 8: *ramok* instead of *ryumok*.

The *TG* and *AM* versions have a dedication to the sculptor E. Neizvestny.

Batu Khan, the grandson of Genghis Khan, conquered Russia in 1236–40.

NEGROES SING

Published in *Z* (No. 4, 1962), *TG,* and *SCA* with some variants. Our text is from *TG*.

The only significant variant is the omission, in *SCA*, of the line "We Negroes, we poets." This line was singled out by the critic V. Nazarenko (*Zvezda*, No. 6, 1962), who insinuated that when Voznesensky writes about oppressed Negroes in America, he is also speaking about the fate of poets in Russia.

NEW YORK BIRD

Published with insignificant variants in *Z* (No. 4, 1962), *TG, SCA,* and *AM*. Our text is from *AM*.

"In Chicago" renders *na Michigane*, which may be interpreted to mean "on Lake Michigan," and thus, by extension, Chicago—a city visited by Voznesensky in 1961.

The poet's companion, in the last stanza, is apparently Evgeni Evtushenko, who accompanied Voznesensky on his visit to the United States in 1961.

ITALIAN GARAGE

Published with some variants in *Yunost* (No. 1, 1963), and *AM*. Our text is from *AM*. Bella Akhmadulina, to whom the poem is dedicated, is a Russian poetess.

6   I'M A FAMILY OF SEVEN

I'M A FAMILY OF SEVEN ...

Published in *SCA* and *TG*, with variants in punctuation. Our text is from *SCA*. The poem is dedicated to J.-P. Sartre.

In *SCA* the poem appears as a "P.S." In *TG* the poem is published without a title under the heading "Avtootstuplenie" ("Autodigression").

A fragment of this poem is given in *AM* as an epigraph to the section of the volume entitled "Sneg pakhnet antonovkoi" ("The Snow Smells of Antonov Apples").

THE NOSE

Published in *AM*. The Russian title is "Ballada-Dissertatsiya" ("Ballad-Dissertation"). For "Buggins," see note on "Hunting a Hare."

YOU LIVE WITH YOUR AUNT ...

Published in *M* and *SCA* with no variants.

Suzdal is an ancient town near Vladimir where Voznesensky spent part of his childhood.

ODE TO GOSSIPS

Published in *P* and *AM* with some variants. Our text is from *AM*.

LILAC TREE

Published in identical form in *Z* (No. 11, 1963) and *AM*. In *AM* the poem has no title and is indexed by first line.

LAZINESS

Published in *Z* (No. 6, 1965).

PARIS WITHOUT RHYME

Published with some variants in *Z* (No. 11, 1963) and *AM*. Our text is from *AM*.

The poet writes in a note to the poem in *Z*: "At the moment Paris is being 'cleaned.' They are taking the top layer off the façades, renovating the city. In the newspapers, in the salons, in the streets, there is a fierce debate pro and con! Romantics complain that the ancient charm of the city is disappearing, that something is being lost which is undefinable, but without which Paris is not Paris. This may be. . . .

"Seeing the outer layer being removed from buildings, I suddenly had the idea of taking the operation a stage further—to look at the city and all the things in it without their exteriors, to look inside! . . .

"I've tried to do this as a realistic fantasy in the good old tradition of Gogol, Swift, or of Pushkin's dream of Tatyana."

The poem begins with three conventionally rhymed quatrains and then, as the city it describes loses its outer forms, the poem breaks into blank verse. The poem reverts to rhyme only toward the end, when the city's walls are restored.

"Douche Charcot" is a medical treatment, named after the French neurologist Jean M. Charcot (1825–93), which consists in directing powerful jets of water on the patient's body.

"Madame Lanchon" is Monique Lanchon, who was in charge of the French government's cultural exchange program with the USSR during Voznesensky's visit to Paris in 1962.

7   OZA

OZA

Published in full in *Molodaya gvardiya*, No. 10, 1964. Excerpts from the poem appeared in *Literaturnaya gazeta*, October 31, 1964.

In *Literaturnaya gazeta* Voznesensky wrote the following note: " 'Oza' is written in the form of a diary left by somebody in a hotel. Oza is the name of the heroine.

"The poems alternate with prose passages which describe the alien world of soul-less 'programmed animals,' hostile to man.

"In art, evil has often taken a phantasmagoric form. I have tried to follow this tradition. The basic theme is interspersed with monologues by a Physicist, a Historian, a Raven, a Poet. . . ."

The Russian text published in this volume differs in some respects from the *Molodaya gvardiya* text. The changes, which involve transpositions of some parts of the poem, and the omission of a few passages, have been made in accordance with a version recited by the poet during his visit to England in 1965. The editors believe that the changes—few of which are substantial—make for greater coherence and unity of the poem. They feel justified, therefore, in following the recited version, rather than the text as published.

The most important differences between our text and *MG* are as follows.

The poem beginning *Ave, Oza* ("Hail, Oza"), which appears at the end of our text (p. 108), is, in *MG*, at the beginning of the work (p. 11).

The passage beginning *Lyublyu ya Dubnu* ("I love Dubna") appears immediately following *Ave, Oza* (p. 12) of the *MG* text.

Three lines of prose on p. 16 of *MG* have been omitted, beginning with *Issinya* and ending with *karniza*.

The line *A pochemy zh, zabyv luga i sosnyaki* ("And why, forgetting meadows and pine groves") in *MG*, p. 18, has been changed to *A pochemy zh, zapolniv Luzhniki* ("And why, packing the Luzhniki"). This change also conforms to the text as published in *Literaturnaya gazeta*.

Two misprints on p. 19 of *MG* have been corrected: the name Kheinman has been changed to Feynman; 1963 has been changed to 1961.

Two lines of verse have been omitted from *MG*, p. 21: *No mashina myslit . . . / no ona myslit mysl'yu ch'ei? Cheloveka!* ("But machines are also able to think / But whose thoughts do they think? Man's!").

Section IX, pp. 25–26 of *MG*, beginning with *Drug* and ending with *golosok*, has been transferred to the beginning and has become Section I.

The final phrase of the last paragraph of p. 27 of *MG*, beginning with *a on* and ending with *yurodivogo*, has been omitted. The words *Borisov, aspirant* on this page have also been omitted.

The seventeen-line passage on p. 29 of *MG*, beginning with *Ty-to* and ending with *ozera*, has been omitted.

The last two lines of the first stanza in Section XII, on p. 32 of *MG*, have been omitted: *Tekhnika v dobrykh rukakh—dobra, / a yesli v zlykh? . . .* ("Technology is good in good hands, / but in bad?").

Eight lines on p. 33 of *MG*, beginning with *Izvinyayus'* and ending with *cheloveka*, have been omitted.

Section XIII, pp. 34–35 of *MG*, has been omitted.

Section I

"Oza" is an anagram of the Russian Christian name Zoya, which is derived from the Greek word for life, *zōē*. The heroine of the poem—the person to whom it is addressed—appears always to be in danger of being transformed or distorted, either by the cyclotron or by the circumstances of her life, into a person beyond the reach of the poet who loves her.

"Stop, moment, you are beautiful!" is a quotation from Goethe's *Faust*.

The "bracelet" worn by Oza-Zoya is a sign of her recklessness. Wearing metal near a cyclotron is strictly against regulations.

Section II

"A Genoese tower": Russians associate towers with Genoa, because of the fortifications built in the Crimea, notably in Feodosya, during its occupation by the Genoese.

Section IV

". . . when we pack the Luzhniki" is a reference to the historic poetry reading in November 1962 in Moscow's Luzhniki Sports Stadium, where 14,000 people gathered to hear Voznesensky, Bella Akhmadulina, and Boris Slutsky.

Mayakovsky committed suicide in 1930 by shooting himself.

"Army commanders aged eighteen" is a reference to the extreme youth of some commanders in the Red Army during the early days of the Civil War.

"We are the earth's first love" is the final line of Boris Pasternak's poem "On the Anniversary of October" ("K oktyabr'skoi godovshchine").

"Socialism, live, human, and true, is now coming about" is a quotation from Mayakovsky.

The poem about Stalin, "Does a high wind make me reel . . . ," is the first satirical treatment of this subject to appear in print in the Soviet Union. The line "Of Stalin do not sing" echoes Pushkin's lines "Do not sing, my beauty, / Songs of sad Georgia" (*Ne poi, krasavitsa, pri mne / Ty pesen' Gruzii pechal'noi*).

"I love Dubna. I have friends there" alludes to the interest and sympathy many of Russia's most important scientists have shown for the new literature of the post-Stalin era. Dubna is the site of one of Russia's largest atomic research installations.

"The author's an abstractionist—take him away!" refers to the campaign against abstract art in 1963. As a result, "abstractionist" became a common, but by no means clearly understood, term of abuse.

Section VI

This parody of Poe's "The Raven" is evidently a dialogue between the author and his alter ego.

"What the hell!" renders *na figa*, the usual printed euphemism for *na huya* ("Oh, fuck!"), with which the preceding line always rhymes.

Section X

The birthday party takes place in Moscow's Hotel Berlin (formerly the Savoy), which has a banquet room with a mirror on the ceiling.

The "I" is Voznesensky himself. He introduces himself in the role of a buffoon, but for a serious purpose. In this sense, he is using the same device as Blok, who introduced himself as Harlequin in his play *The Black Rose*.

The "prayer" is addressed to the icon of the Blessed Virgin of Vladimir, one of the great thaumaturgical icons of Russia.

Section XI

The fourth and fifth stanzas allude to the attacks on Voznesensky in 1963 (see Introduction), when he was prohibited from giving public readings.

Section XII

The "mechanical nightingale" in the fourth stanza echoes the legend about an emperor who, being dissatisfied with the natural song of the nightingale, had a mechanical bird made for himself. W. B. Yeats used the same image to distinguish between natural and artificial song in the last stanza of "Sailing to Byzantium."

In the fifth stanza, "Rublev, Blok, and Lenin" represent an apparently incongruous assemblage of names. At first sight it would seem that the fourteenth-century icon painter, the symbolist poet, and the author of the October Revolution have little in common. They are perhaps intended to suggest varying aspects of the Russian spirit—among these, Orthodox religiosity, poetic sensibility, and a capacity for narrow devotion to an ideal, whatever it may be.

In the lines "And all the bushes are tinkling with berries. / In their clear sound I shall not die," the berries are probably rowan berries (*ryabina*). These winter berries are known in the folklore of several countries as a symbol of life in death. This motif figures in Pasternak's *Doctor Zhivago*, Chapter 12.